REXOLOGY

THE WAY OF A WARRIOR IN THE NEW MILLENNIUM

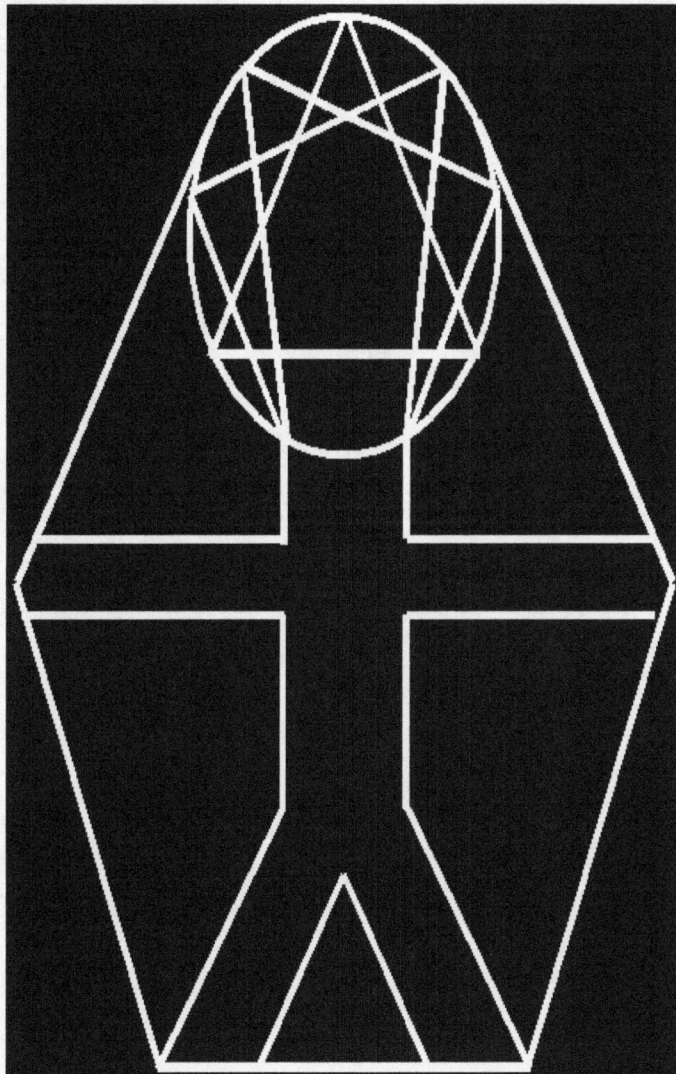

Reginald W. Davis

REXOLOGY

The Way of a Warrior in the New Millennium

By

Reginald W. Davis

Published by

Rexology Press
Birmingham, Alabama
http://www.RexologyPress.com

Front Cover Design, Illustrations and Tables

By

Reginald W. Davis

Cover Photos: Hubble Ultra Deep Field

Courtesy of NASA and the Space Telescope Science Institute

SECOND EDITION

Published by

Rexology Press

Birmingham, Alabama

http://www.RexologyPress.com

ISBN: 978-0-6151-4566-2

Library of Congress Control Number: 2007928587

DEDICATION

I proudly dedicate this book with love and appreciation to my parents (Oreadus and Tommie Davis), my aunt (Juanita Kitt), my friend (Robert Bren), my kids (Reginald and Rachel), and to the Church and Community of Friendship, Alabama, USA.

CONTENTS

List of Illustrations

Foreword

It is human nature to wonder, to reason, and to act. They are natural drives, like sex and hunger. Wondering and inductive logic gave rise to myth, philosophy, and science through "cosmological convictions." This means having a deep belief in the order of the universe. Myth or mysticism deals with the most basic beliefs, concepts, and attitudes of an individual or group. It is the belief that one can attain direct knowledge of God through subjective experiences, such as intuition or insight. It asserts that God, or the gods, gave order to the universe. It place people at the center of the cosmos, examples are:

1. "The Genesis Story" as told in the Bible.

2. The Babylonians "Enuma Elish" - the gods created humans to serve them.

3. The Babylonians "Gilgamesh Epic" - no eternal life, do what you have to do.

Philosophy is a way of life, or a system of values by which one lives - based on intellectual means and moral self-discipline. Philosophy asks speculative questions in a logical order, and yields rational answers through reflective thinking - reason. This leaves us open rationally to the many possibilities in life. Other benefits of philosophy include:

1. It helps us to understand people of different times.

2. It teaches us how to make decisions when we are not sure.

3. It helps us to see why we act the way we do.

4. It has tools to help us make value judgments more rationally.

Science is the study of the nature and behavior of the physical universe. In science, you observe and experiment. This leads to the objective discovery of natural laws that affect the whole universe. This takes humans away from the center of the cosmos. Aristotle (384-322 BC) was an ancient Greek philosopher, and the scientist who founded physics. He was a student of Plato (427-347 BC) and the teacher of Alexander the Great (356-323 BC). Aristotle asserted that all knowledge must begin with observation. However, in his natural philosophy, God functioned as the final cause of condition for the cosmos. This view represented the scientific community until about 1600 AD.

Galileo Galilee (1564-1642) was an Italian naturalist philosopher, mathematician, physicist, and astronomer. He is the "father of modern astronomy," and the "father of modern physics." He asserted that all knowledge comes from observation. However, you cannot observe God. In addition, measurements are quantitative. This mean we do not have to know the final cause of motion and change. The scientific world is a secular or non-religious world. Science asserts there is no super natural destiny. Man is a part of nature, which is not divine. Do you have cosmological convictions? How do you express them in your life? Should science replace myth and philosophy - why or why not?

In life, I found many people who thought their way was the right way. As a Christian, I wondered, "How do you tell and convince others that Jesus Christ is the way?" This led to my question, "With all the different thoughts, beliefs, religions, and sciences; how do you know what path to follow in order to find self-actualization (The fulfillment of your total potential) and spiritual-fulfillment (Having values and beliefs, as to right and wrong, such that you are willing to live or die for)?" In order to find the answer, you must look both within yourself and without. By examining yourself objectively, you begin to understand yourself. This leads to the understanding of others. By looking outward objectively, you begin to understand your relationship to the world around you and your possibilities in it.

"REXOLOGY: The Way of a Warrior in the New Millennium" is about the search for truth, knowledge, and understanding. Understanding the knowledge you have acquired gives you the ability to apply it. This ability to apply knowledge makes you "a person of knowledge and power." Becoming a person of knowledge and power will lead you to new levels of consciousness. As you increase your consciousness, you increase your capacity to accept and handle both knowledge and power.

This is a book of esoteric knowledge. By definition, this is knowledge of the few. However, for those who can hear and understand it may unlock their full potential. It will help you to develop, or become more aware of your beliefs and convictions. In addition, it will help you to see who and what you truly are.

Introduction

Reginald W. Davis is a "Certified Biomedical Engineering Technician" in Birmingham, Alabama, USA. His certification is through the Association for the Advancement of Medical Instrumentation (AAMI), and the International Certification Commission (ICC) for clinical engineering and biomedical technology. In addition, he has a certification through the Radiological Service Training Institute as a "Diagnostic Imaging Instrumentation Specialist." He is responsible for the comprehensive technical support of highly sophisticated scientific apparatus, including biomedical and laboratory instrumentation systems.

Reginald was born in a small country community called Friendship. It is located about twenty-five miles northwest of Montgomery, Alabama. The date was Sunday, January 12, 1958. He grew up in a Christian environment, went to church, and believed in Jesus Christ from an early age. As a Christian, he believed that God was the only true reality; and that Jesus Christ was the truth, the light, and the way. Any other approach to reality or cosmology was a delusion.

Around the age of fifteen, he met a man who introduced him to the concept of esoteric knowledge. They talked about things like the Trigrams, the Upanishads, and the Kabbalah. The Trigrams are an ancient Chinese art. It promotes balance and harmony in ones living and working conditions. The Upanishads are a collection of Hindu text with emphasis on the nature of reality and the soul. The Kabbalah is an oral tradition of Jewish Mysticism, which dates back to the 12th century BC. It was during this time that he first heard the word "Tetragrammaton." This is the four Hebrew letters, "Yod, He, Waw, He." This corresponds to YHWH (Yahweh) or JHVH (Jehovah).

Reginald has always pursued the development of himself physically, mentally, and spiritually. At the age of twelve, he learned to play the saxophone. In high school, he played basketball and football. While in the military, he studied yoga and the martial arts. After the military, he took classes in psychology and philosophy. He put emphases on trying to classify things in a logical and coherent manner. While at the same time, he was trying to put things together in such a way that it would be consistent and meaningful to the intuitive mind. At this point, he started collecting his notes, which lead to the formulation of this book, "REXOLOGY: The Way of a Warrior in the New Millennium."

Chapter One

A Person of Knowledge and Power

Sir Francis Bacon (1561-1626), the father of deductive reasoning, was an English lawyer and philosopher. At the dawn of the Scientific Age in 1597, he asserted, "Knowledge is Power." Knowledge by definition is, 1) what an individual knows, or can learn, and 2) What humanity knows, or can learn. Power by definition is a position of control, authority, or influence. In addition, it is the ability to act or produce an effect. Therefore, power is the ability to apply knowledge.

"A person of knowledge and power" is someone who seeks truth, knowledge, and understanding. Understanding the knowledge you have acquired, gives you the ability to apply it. This ability to apply knowledge makes you a person of knowledge and power. However, knowledge in itself does not equate to understanding. It is possible to know something, and yet not understand. Understanding comes with diversity. When we can see a thing from more then one point of view, our understanding of it is increased. You may know something intellectually; but until you can sense and feel the things connected with it, there is no true understanding. Truth must be lived. There are levels of understanding that come only over a period of time - sometime years.

Becoming a person of knowledge and power is an on going process, or never ending struggle. By definition a warrior is, 1) a person engaged, or experienced in warfare, and 2) A person engaged in a struggle or conflict. Because life itself is a struggle, each of us is a warrior by default. We have a physical struggle for our material needs - such as food, clothing, and shelter. We have an emotional struggle for our values and beliefs. We have an intellectual struggle for the acquisition of knowledge and understanding.

A person of knowledge and power is a warrior, who lives a warrior's life. This obligates you to have an aesthetic attitude toward your experiences. This means viewing life in terms of your values and beliefs, and living accordingly. Affection, loyalty, self-sacrifice, honor, and a sense of shame are the core values of a warrior. These values give order and direction to life. Having respect put things in a meaningful perspective. This leads to emotional stability, and self-discipline.

Carlos Castaneda (1925-1998), born in Peru, was an author and anthropologist. In his book, "The Teachings of Don Juan," Don Juan asserted, "A man of knowledge is one who has followed truthfully the hardships of learning. A man who has, without rushing or without faltering, gone as far as he can in unraveling the secrets of power and knowledge." Don Juan was a Yaqui Indian. The Yaqui are a border Native American people who originally lived throughout the Sonoran Desert, from northern Mexico to Arizona.

Don Juan was also a Shaman. His teachings included a form of sorcery and black magic through hallucinogenic plants (peyote, jimson weed, and mushrooms). By definition, Shamanism is a magical-religious phenomenon. It is a means, or use of supernatural power to influence natural forces. Its' focus is on an ecstatic trance like state of being. This is a state beyond reason and self-control. It has overwhelming emotions such as joy, fear, rage, or awe. In this state, the soul of the shaman is believed to leave the body (an out-of-body experience), and ascends to the sky (heavens), or descends into the earth (underworld).

Don Juan goes on to say, "He (a man) must challenge and defeat his four natural enemies. A man can call himself a man of knowledge only if he is capable of defeating all four of them." Your four natural enemies are "Fear," "Clarity of Mind," "Power," and "Old Age and Death."

Learning can and will lead to the unexpected. Being unexpected it can be intimidating. Along with negative emotions, it can create fear. Fear is the first and worst of your four natural enemies. It shoots adrenalin into the body, but it can also freeze you helpless to one spot. It is a basic emotional sensation that causes apprehension, concerns, or regret over an unwanted situation. A perceived risk or threat is what usually initiates fear. It can vary from a mild caution to an extreme phobia. However, fear can be useful as a warning of a potentially dangerous or dreadful situation or consequence.

Fear gives power to the things you fear. It allows them to control you as opposed to you controlling them. It can even affect your self-image or self-concept, and hinder your pursuit for self-actualization. When you conquer your fear, you become authentic. You enable yourself to feel and act freely from your essence. This is what it means to be ones' self.

To overcome your fears, you must be able to identify and deal with them. Ask yourself, "Why am I afraid?" Make an honest assessment and create a plan of action. You must face your fears and go on in spite of them. Moreover, a time will come when your first enemy will be no more. "Yea, though I walk through the valley of the shadow of death, I will fear no evil: for thou art with me; thy rod and thy staff they comfort me. (Psalm 23:4)"

Once fear is conquered, you begin to see things in a different light. You find yourself experiencing clarity of mind. However, now you will have stumbled upon your second natural enemy. Clarity refers to one's ability to visualize an object or concept as it really is. Clarity of mind is the ability to assess the situations and circumstances as they really are. This ability to see things as they really are helps you to make sound judgments. This leads to self-confidence. At this point, you begin to claim knowledge as power. "Then the eyes of those who see will no longer be closed, and the ears of those who hear will listen. The mind of the rash will know and understand, and the stammering tongue will be fluent and clear. No longer will the fool be called noble nor the scoundrel be highly respected. (Isaiah 32:3-5)"

Because your situations and circumstances continuously change, achieving clarity of mind is an ongoing process. Never the less, your clarity compels you to complete confidence in yourself, and you become bold in your actions. However, you must exercise control over your clarity. Use it to observe, and wait patiently for the right moment to act. A time will come when you will realize that your clarity was only a moment in time. Thus, you will have over come your second natural enemy.

Your third natural enemy is "Power!" Most people who have acquired power, commands. They begin by taking calculated risks, and end in making rules. The problem is, once people start acquiring power, they tend to set themselves apart from, and above others. They begin to view themselves with admiration. However, you must come to understand that this power is in reality not yours. At that moment you will know when and how to use power. Thus, you will have defeated your third natural enemy.

Personal power is real power, but only through the grace of God. Psalms 62:11 tell us, "Power is God's." Therefore, God the creator is the ultimate source of all power, knowledge, and wisdom. It is His to distribute as He wills. "To one is given the word of wisdom ... to another the word of knowledge ... to another faith ... to another the gifts of healing ... But one and the same Spirit works all these things, giving to each individual as He wills. (1 Corinthians 12: 8-9)"

Your fourth natural enemy is "Old age and Death." Old age is the latter period of life, and death is a part of the physiological process. They will come to us all. Many people fear the problems that are associated with old age (dementia, poverty, health care a lack of Medicare insurance, loneliness, depression). However, old age can be productive and vital, with a great deal of happiness. If one has prepared them selves, they will come into old age with knowledge and understanding. They will be ready for both suffering and happiness.

Death is the natural ending to life. You can prolong life, but you cannot deny death. Modern medical science can prolong life with medical technology, but it cannot stop death from coming. Proverbs 10:27 states, "The fear of the Lord prolongeth days: but the years of the wicked shall be shortened." James 5:15 states, "And the prayer of faith shall save the sick, and the Lord shall raise him up..." You will not be able to defeat your last natural enemy; but if you can fight it off, at that moment you will have become a true person of knowledge and power. A person is only defeated when they give up, and no longer tries.

Don Juan asserted that drama, or "controlled folly" is the single most outstanding issue in the path of a man of knowledge. A controlled folly is more then acting. "It is a profound state of belief." It means playing the role that one wants to become, with understanding and sincere feelings. Over a period, you find this role has become a part of you. This is a demonstration of applied knowledge and the use of power. To play to perfection any desired role in your external life while inwardly remaining free. This drama represents the perfection of a person of knowledge and power.

One last proposition of Don Juan's system was "stopping the world." Don Juan asserted, "The ordinary world is only a description maintained by social consensus and internal dialogue. Stop the dialogue and we can see the other reality and learn another description of the world." This is a form of meditation. It quiets and relaxes the mind, which allows you to perceive things in a non-ordinary manor.

In summary, a person of knowledge and power is someone who seeks truth, knowledge, and understanding. Understanding the knowledge you have acquired gives you the ability to apply it. This ability to apply knowledge makes you a person of knowledge and power. However, this is a never-ending struggle, and this struggle makes you a warrior, which is a way of life. Being a warrior obligates you to live in terms of your values and beliefs.

We are all warriors at heart. It is simply a matter of how we see ourselves, and how we choose to live our lives. If one decides to become a person of knowledge and power, they must be willing to live accordingly. On the path of true development, something old must die in a person, and something new must be born in them. You have to abandon what you have learned, and reconstruct everything for yourself. This is the process of developing a conscious soul.

As a person of knowledge and power, you must challenge and defeat your four natural enemies. Your four natural enemies are "Fear," "Clarity of Mind," "Power," and "Old age and Death." Once you have defeated all four of them, at that point you will have become a true person of knowledge and power.

God, the Father, gives power and gifts to us all, based on our capacity to handle it. An eight-ounce cup can only hold eight ounces of water. More power then you can handle could be very dangerous to you and the people around you. With only a partial understanding, a person can be a threat to themselves and others. However, once you reach a certain level of understanding, the misuse of power becomes impossible.

Becoming a person of knowledge and power will lead you to new levels of consciousness. Here are "four tasks" that will help you to accomplish this goal:

1. The "first task" is to come to know self. Your concept of who you are determines how you perceive and relate to the world. Chapter 2, "Self and Human Nature," describes this task.

2. The "second task" is to develop your consciousness. As you increase your consciousness, you increase your capacity to accept and handle both knowledge and power. Chapter 3, "The Four Ways to Consciousness," describes this task. It also describes several techniques of meditation, which allows us to experience things in a fuller way. In addition, it includes a technique called "self-remembering." Self-remembering enables you to feel and act freely from your essence. This is what it means to be ones' self.

3. The "third task" is to interact with the world around you on a conscious level. You become an observer of yourself, and learn about yourself, as you learn about the world around you. Chapter 4, "The Three Areas of Human Experience," describes this task.

4. The "fourth task" is to learn to see yourself, and the world around you, from a cosmological point of view. A true cosmological point of view will allow you to satisfy your

threefold nature of body, soul, and spirit (regardless of your religion). Chapter 5, "Cosmology and Cosmological Convictions," describes this task.

Chapter Two

Self and Human Nature

The "first task" of a person of knowledge and power is to come to know one's self. Our concept of who we are determines how we perceive and relate to the world. The self-concept is the organized set of characteristics that we perceive as being peculiar to an individual, based on the evaluation of our social experiences. According to Carl Rogers (1902-1987), our self-concept directs our behavior, and determines how we see reality. Although our image of our self, such as strong or weak, may or may not correspond to the way others see us. Rogers was an influential American psychologist. He developed a humanistic theory of personality, which included his view of the self and the human condition, and his rationale for the improvement of this condition.

Rogers' theory emphasized the concept of "self-actualization." This implies that there is an internal, biological drive to learn, to grow, and to develop one's capacities and talents to the fullest. He thought that people who were "brought up" in an environment of unconditional positive regard (a general acceptance, and appreciation of who they are) had the best opportunity of developing a positive self-view, and reaching self-actualization.

Throughout history, there have been many definitions of self. Plato (427-347 BC) was a very influential Greek philosopher. He was the student of Socrates (469-347 BC) and the teacher of Aristotle (384-322 BC). Plato asserted that people are a duality - the physical and the non-physical. The body is the physical component of each person, and the soul is the non-physical component. He believed that these two components exist separately and independent of each other. However, the soul resides within the physical body. In addition, the soul has three parts (see Figure 2-1):

1. The Mind (The King or Reason)
2. The Emotions (The Appetite – Bad)
3. The Will (The Spirit or Warrior – Good)

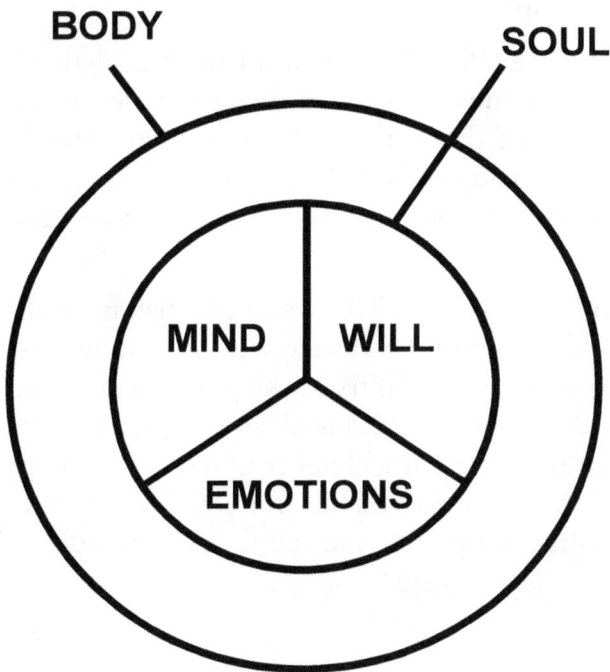

Figure 2-1: Plato's concept of self

Rene Descartes (1596-1650), also known as Cartesius, was a noted French philosopher, mathematician, skeptic, and scientist. He was one of the key thinkers of the Scientific Age. He is the "Founder of Modern Philosophy" and the "Father of Modern Mathematics." He developed a theory called Cartesian Dualism. In this theory, there are two fundamental types of material in the world - the physical or body, and the nonphysical or mind. Descartes associated the mind with consciousness and self-awareness. He asserted that the self is the thinker. It is private, individual, and unobservable. It is a thing of conscious substance. Self is eternal, and do not change. The body is not important. The real person is inside. Self is nonphysical.

Gilbert Ryle (1900-1976) was a British analytic philosopher, known for his critique of Cartesian dualism. Ryle rejected Descartes, and said Descartes did not use the language right, that he made a logical error. Ryle said self is collective. It is all of you and your behavior. You are what you do. Self is not a private entity, but public.

David Hume (1711-1776) was a Scottish naturalist, economist, and historian. He developed the bundle theory of the self. This suggests that if you try looking within yourself (introspection), all you will find is ideas, feelings, perceptions, and changing impressions. You will never perceive anything that you could call "I", or the owner of this bundle. Therefore, there is no self. He thought what people call self is only a bundle of sensations and perceptions (see Figure 2-2).

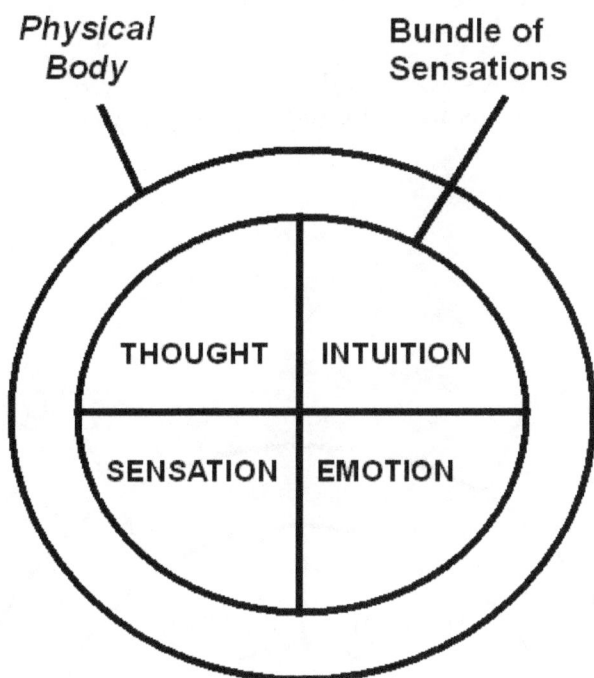

Figure 2-2: David Hume's concept of self

Carl Jung (1875-1961) was a world-renowned psychiatrist from Switzerland, and the founder of analytical psychology. His most famous theory is the theory of the Collective Unconscious. This is a universal reservoir of experiences common to all human beings. His theory includes the concept of archetypes; this is the original pattern or model, which is used to make every thing else of the same type. In psychology, an archetype is a model of a person, personality, or behavior.

Jung asserted that the self is an archetype symbolizing the whole of the personality. For Jung the ego is the center of consciousness, and the self is the center of the total psyche, including both the conscious and the unconscious. He asserted self is a bundle of sensations, but this bundle has self-awareness. It is what make up or constitute the individuality and identity of a person (see Figure 2-3).

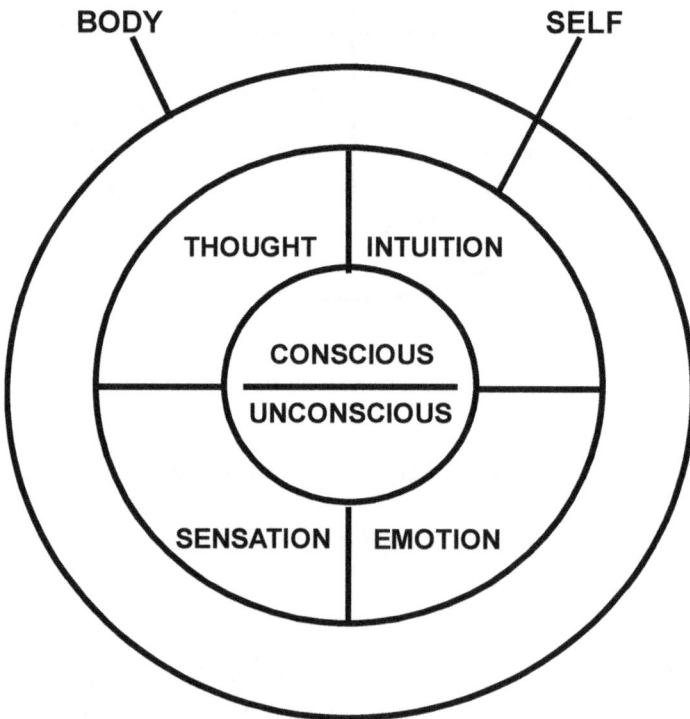

Figure 2-3: Carl Jung's concept of self

Burrhus Frederic (B. F.) Skinner (1904-1990) was an American psychologist and author. He developed the theory of operant conditioning - the idea that you can shape or determine behavior through positive and negative reinforcements. He denied the existence of a mind as a thing separate from the body, and asserted:

1. There is no inner self, only body and heredity.

2. There are only positive and negative enforcements in our environment. These have an affect on our attitude and our behavior.

3. There is no freedom of choice. Our genes and life's enforcements determine our course of action.

William James (1842-1910) was an American psychologist, and philosopher. He asserted that self is the sum total of what you are. This includes your mind, your body, your friends, your family, your job, and your possessions. He asserted there are two aspects of self. The first aspect of self is the self as subject, the knower, or the "I." However, he thought there is no need for a metaphysical "I" - the thinker. He concluded that the thought itself was the thinker. The second aspect of self is the self as object, the known, or the "Me." He said there are three basic types of the "Me:" the "material me," the "social me," and the "spiritual me."

The Bible tells us, "… And may your spirit and soul and body be kept strong … (1 Thessalonians 5:23)" This tells us that we are composed of three separate parts: a spirit, a soul, and a body (see Figure 2-4). The body or "The Physical Man" is the material part of a person (your flesh and blood). The soul or "The Soul Man" is the nonphysical or psychological part of a person. It is self-aware, and has its own personality and identity that separates it from others. It is the mind, the will, and the emotions of a person. The spirit or "The Spirit Man" is the supernatural essence of a person. "It is the essence of our consciousness." It is the breath of life. It is what makes the human being a living person. It is a spark from God's eternal flame.

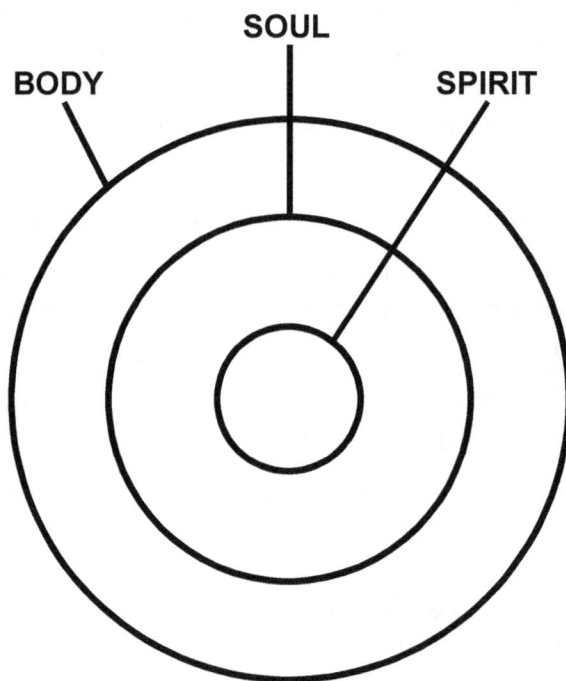

Figure 2-4: The Bible's concept of self

Descartes' used the "Argument from Analogy" to prove that other selves outside of his own existed. An analogy is an inference that if different things have some characteristics in common, they may have other similar characteristics. The question is how do you know anything about another person's inner experiences, or even if they have inner experiences at all? He reasoned that when he hurt himself, he felt pain, and gave off expressions of pain. Therefore, when you hurt yourself, and give off expressions of pain, it is safe to assume that you also feel pain. We can infer from outside behavior what is inside of us.

Acknowledging that there are other selves brings about the question of how to relate to them. Martin Buber (1878-1965) was a philosopher, translator, and educator from Austria. He believed what defines human existence is the way we communicate or relate with each other, with the world, and with God. He asserted human beings adopt one of two attitudes toward their relationships, either the "I-Thou (you)" attitude or the "I-It" attitude. He emphasized the importance of the "I - Thou" attitude. This is an attitude of openness, and respect toward others. Being personally involved is real human life. The "I - IT" attitude emphasizes a logical and detached point of view. It is a form of science - detach, study, and control.

Human Nature refers to the fundamental dispositions and traits of human beings. The Bible defines human nature as, 1) "The heart is deceitful above all things, and desperately wicked. (Jeremiah 17:9)," and 2) "The carnal (natural) mind is enmity (hostile) against God; for it is not subject to the law of God, neither indeed can be. (Romans 8:7)" By these definitions, human nature is not very nice.

Sigmund Freud (1856-1939) was an Austrian neurologist and the founder of the psychoanalytic school of psychology. He believed the things that drive people are unconscious animalistic and instinctual urges, particularly lust and aggression. He proposed that the psyche (self or mind) has three parts: the ego, the super-ego, and the id. The id contains "primitive desires" (hunger, rage, and sex), the super-ego contains internalized norms, morality and taboos, and the ego mediates between the two and may include or give rise to the sense of self.

Jean-Paul Sartre (1905-1980) was a French existentialist and atheist. He asserted there is no divine creator, and that human beings have no metaphysical or supernatural destiny. His view of human responsibility included:

1. Each of us is finally and completely responsible for who, and what we are. We are responsible for our actions, and for what we become.

2. Antagonism between people occurs because we treat each other like things. We try to control them, or they try to control us.

3. "We are condemned to be free." We are required to make choices and to accept responsibility for their consequences.

Abraham Maslow (1908-1970) was an American existentialist. He developed a theory called "Maslow's Hierarchy of Needs." He asserted that individuals have to satisfy their basic needs before they are motivated to pursue self-actualization (the fulfillment of ones total potential). He asserted there are five different levels of human needs (see Table 2-1). The first two levels of needs are "basic needs." The third level of need is "social motives." This indicates there are no real hermits. The last two levels of needs are "competence or motivation needs."

Table 2-1:

Abraham Maslow's hierarchy of human needs

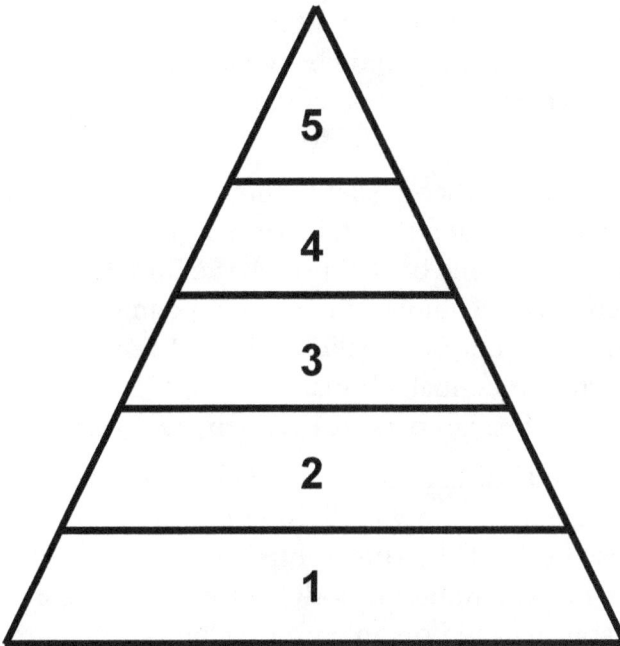

1. **Physiological Needs:** The need to satisfy hunger, thirst, and sex drives.

2. **Safety Needs:** This is the need to feel safe, secure, and out of danger.

3. **Belonging and Love Needs:** This is the need to affiliate with others, to be accepted, and to belong.

4. **Esteem Needs:** This is the need to achieve, to be competent, to gain approval, and to be recognized.

5. **Self-Actualization Needs:** This is the need to fulfill one's unique potentials.

In summary, the "first task" of a person of knowledge and power is to come to know one's self. Carl Rogers asserted our self-concept directs our behavior, and that it determines how we see reality. Throughout history, there have been many definitions of self. There are even those who say there is no inner self, only body and heredity. If you try looking within yourself, all you will find is ideas, feelings, perceptions, and changing impressions. You will never perceive anything that you could call "I", or the owner of this bundle.

Psychoanalytic theories and Humanistic theories are both valid ways of approaching the study of personality. Psychoanalytic theories emphasize some of the more basic impulses of the human animal, which need restraints. Where as, humanistic theories emphasize how each person make choices of how to live and how to maximize their potential. Humanists assert that the only way to be truly happy is through personal growth and understanding.

Scholars still disagree over the dichotomy (a division into two parts) or the trichotomy (a division into three parts) of a person. Those in the dichotomy camp assert that people are a duality. This includes mind vs. body, essence vs. personality, material vs. spiritual, and organic vs. psychic. Those in the trichotomy camp assert that people are a triune being of spirit, soul, and body. Which camp do you fall in? I believe, "You are a spirit, who has a soul, and live in a body" (see Figure 2-5). Genesis 2:7 states, "And the Lord God formed man of the dust of the ground, and breathed into his nostrils the breath of life; and man became a living soul."

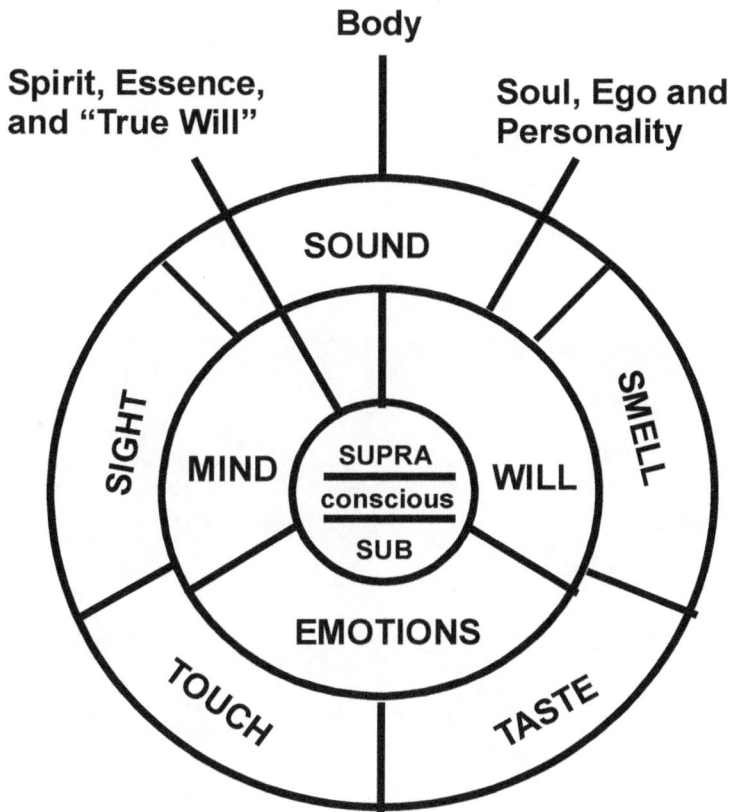

Figure 2-5: Reginald W. Davis' view of self

Chapter Three

The Four Ways to Consciousness

The "second task" of a person of knowledge and power is to develop their consciousness (the quality or state of being aware). As you increase your consciousness, you increase both your knowledge and power. There are two states of consciousness. One is subjective. The other is objective. Subjective consciousness is reality as perceived. It refers to your inner experiences, as you actually experience them - sipping fine wine or listening to music. What you observe may be different from what someone else observes.

Objective consciousness is independent of the state of mind. It is perceptible by all observers. Everyone observes the same thing. Objective knowledge can predict the outcome of an experiment that will be consistent no matter who conduct the experiment. Philosophers and scientists seek "truth" based on the evidence obtained through the physical senses. However, each individual person forms the "truth" in their own mind - subjective knowledge based on sense data.

Sir Karl Popper (1902-1994) was an Austrian-born British philosopher, and a professor at the London School of Economics. He believed that knowledge evolve from experiences of the mind. He proposed a "three world" theory of knowledge, which includes both subjective knowledge and objective knowledge. "World 1" is the physical world, the world of physics. "World 2" is the psychological world, the world of subjective experiences. "World 3" is the world of objective knowledge, the world of the products of the mind. This includes works of music, art, ethical values, technology, and social institutions (society). "It transcends its makers."

Gorge Ivanovitch (G. I.) Gurdjieff (1866? -1949) was a Russian Armenian mystic and teacher of a blend of several Eastern teachings. He asserted that ordinary consciousness is similar to a form of sleep; however, through spiritual discipline and self-observation it is possible to reach new levels of consciousness (both subjective and objective). He believed his teaching was a complete spiritual path leading to consciousness and super consciousness - a form of esoteric psychology, which he called "The Fourth Way."

Peter Demianovich (P. D.) Ouspensky (1878-1947) was a Russian philosopher, mathematician, writer, teacher, mystic and student of Gurdjieff's. In addition, he was one of the major esoteric thinkers of the twentieth century. Ouspensky introduced Gurdjieff's teachings to Western readers in his book "In Search of the Miraculous." In Ouspensky's book, Gurdjieff asserted:

1. Within objective knowledge, there is unity of diversity (The unity of everything).

2. With objective consciousness, it is possible to see and feel the unity of everything.

3. Objective knowledge is knowledge based upon ancient methods and principles of observation.

4. The aim of "myths" was to reach peoples higher emotional centers.

5. The aim of "symbols" was to reach peoples higher thinking centers.

Rodney Collin (1909-1956) was an English writer and student of Ouspensky. In his book, "The Theory of Celestial Influence", Collin described the four ways to consciousness:

1. The first way to consciousness is through the physical functions. This includes both instinctive and motor functions. You gain the ability to control yourself, through difficult physical exercises and body postures. This is the way of the yogi.

2. The second way to consciousness is through the emotional functions. This is the way of faith. It is the way of the monk, or nun.

3. The third way to consciousness is through the intellectual functions. It is changing thought into understanding. It is the way of the philosopher.

4. The fourth way to consciousness consists in mastering the physical functions, the emotional functions, and the intellectual functions all at the same time - simultaneously. This way embraces all sides of a person under ordinary conditions of life.

Collin wrote, "By becoming fully conscious in one function, a man finds his way to consciousness of his whole being: by transforming the nature of this one function, he transforms his whole self…"

The First Way

The first way to consciousness is through the physical functions. Collin asserted the first way is similar to what people in the West call asceticism (the practice of self-denial and abstinence from worldly pleasures, including the denial of physical or psychological desires in order to attain a spiritual goal). The most common ascetic practice is fasting. Many ascetics believe the action of purifying the body helps to purify the soul.

In ancient times, movements of the body played an important role in many cultures. These movements include gymnastics, dance, religious ceremonies, and the martial arts. These movements contain and express certain forms of knowledge, passed from generation to generation. The various types of practice performed in all martial arts produce physical skills. In addition, they still the logical (rational) portion of the brain and allow us to relate to life with other areas of our mind. Both individual form practice and training with a partner constitutes "moving meditation."

These postures and gestures represent and express some universal understanding. They help us to obtain increased levels of sensation; including hearing, sight, touch, taste, and smell. In addition, they help in the development of concentration, patience, and will. Collin wrote, "This is the way of achieving consciousness by mastering physical functions, by overcoming pain. It is the way of transmuting pain into will... and in its full form is known as Hatha Yoga." People who have reached their goal on this path are "Yogis." The goal of Hatha Yoga is complete self-control over both body and mind.

Selvarajan Yesudian (1916-1998) was a yogis and native of India. Elisabeth Haich is a teacher of yoga at the Yogaschule Yesudian-Haich in Europe. In their book "Yoga and Health"

(1953), they wrote, "Our body is enlivened by positive and negative currents, and when these currents are in complete equilibrium, we enjoy perfect health. ... The positive pole is in the top of the skull at the point where our hair forms a whorl. ... The negative pole is in the coccyx, the lowest vertebra. Between these two poles, there is a current of extremely high frequency and short wavelength. This tension is life!"

Between the positive and negative poles, there are five other similar current centers. These current centers, or nerve centers, are charkas in Sanskrit (an ancient Indo-Aryan language). These current centers are points of energy in the astral body. Some people call the astral body the soul. It is the seat of feeling and desire. In addition, the astral body is capable of leaving the physical body for an out-of-body experience. Some people believe these current centers are associated with colors called auras. These auras indicate one's spiritual and physical health. The control of consciousness awakens these current centers. Each level reached opens up a new condition of consciousness for the yogi (see Figure 3-1).

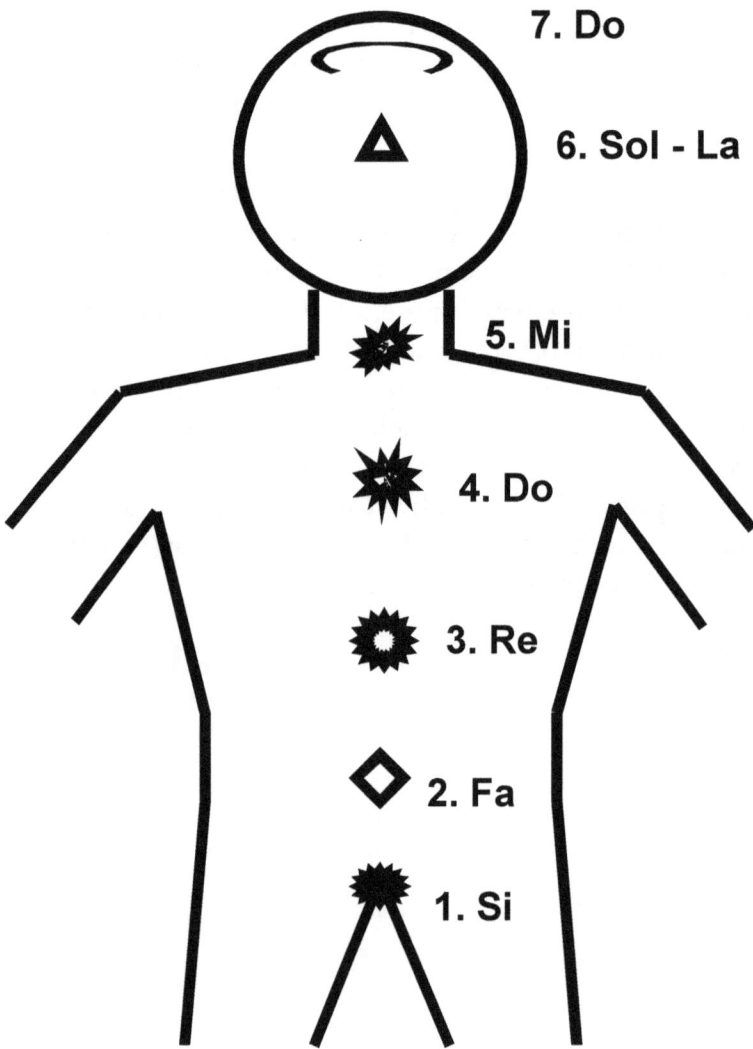

Figure 3-1: The Current Centers

Yesudian and Haich wrote, "One who wants to become a yogi, however, must practice so long that he is able to direct his consciousness to the smallest parts of his body." Our bodies react to the slightest impulses of the mind, and the condition of the body affects our state of mind. Hatha Yoga utilizes this reciprocal relationship, and both mind and body become healthy.

Meditation is the act or process of meditating. When you meditate, you are engaging in a mental exercise (such as concentration on one's breathing or repetition of a mantra) for the purpose of relaxation and awareness. Many groups have used meditation to help them achieve their objects. These groups include the Buddhists, the Taoists, the Shinto, the Sufis, and the Indian Yogis. Meditation makes use of different techniques that help us focus our attention. This aids us in achieving a state of deep calmness, combined with awareness. In this state, our normal ways of thinking and perceiving are suspended, and we experience things in a fuller way.

The different forms of meditation practiced by these groups have certain mental and physical methods in common. Chief among them are muscular-relaxation techniques. One technique used to aid in meditation is the "tension/relaxation technique." The object is to tense and then relax one group of muscles at a time until the entire body is relaxed. Do this as if you were covering your body from feet to head with a sheet. After a while, you will be able to tense every muscle in you body at the same time, hold, and then relax all the muscles simultaneously. The ultimate goal is to be able to relax with no need to tense the muscles - relaxation will have become a conditioned response.

Another technique used to aid in meditation is the "concentrative technique." The gold is to focus your attention exclusively on a single object, an image, a sound or a repeated word or phrase, or a part of the body. An example of this is transcendental meditation (TM). Its aim is a detached frame of mind.

Another form of the concentrative technique is the "opening-up technique". You open yourself to all sensations, such as air moving in and out of the lungs. This focuses your attention, and helps you to relax. In both cases, meditation requires a quiet environment, a relaxed posture, and a positive attitude. People who study yoga and meditation know that there is a direct correlation between one's breath and one's state of the mind. Because of this, if you focus your attention of your breathing, as your breathing becomes slower your mind becomes more at peace and aware.

Tai Chi is an ancient Chinese discipline of "meditative movements" practiced as a system of exercises. Unlike classical yoga, the movements of tai chi are natural to the human body. It increases body flexibility, mind-body coordination, and consciousness. Theses rhythmic movements are slow, smooth flowing, and gentle.

Bruce Tegner (1929-1985) was an American innovator, writer, and teacher of the marshal arts. He held a "Black Belt" in Judo and Karate. He was born in Chicago, Illinois where both his mother and father were professional teachers of judo and jujitsu; they began instructing Bruce in the martial arts when he was only two years old. In the U. S. armed forces, he trained instructors to teach unarmed combat. He also taught military police and coached sport judo teams.

In his book "Kung Fu and Tai Chi" (1968), Tegner wrote, "The purpose of tai chi is to make certain that the mind is present, not absent, during the performance of the movements. ... As you make each move, think about it: let your mind dwell on the form, the shape, and the body's posture. Awareness is involvement of the conscious senses and being aware of what you are doing ... Because there is no competition involved, tai chi promotes a relaxed mental attitude, which transfers to relax the body. ... Coordination of eye-limb activity involves a degree of mental concentration, which is stimulating and relaxing. Flexibility, grace and lightness of movement, and emotional refreshment can result from earnest and diligent practice of tai chi."

In Summary, the first way to consciousness is through the physical functions. Through difficult physical exercises and body postures, you gain the ability to control yourself. This is the way of the yogi. The goal is complete self-control over both body and mind. Hatha Yoga teaches life force is the flow of positive and negative currents of extremely high frequency and short wavelength in the body. There are seven current centers in the body. The control of consciousness awakens these current centers. Each level reached opens up a new level of consciousness for the yogi.

Meditation is the act or process of meditating. People meditate for the purpose of relaxation and awareness. Meditation makes use of different techniques that help us focus our attention. This aids us in achieving a state of deep calmness, combined with awareness. Because there is a direct correlation between one's breath and one's state of the mind, if you focus your attention of your breathing, you will find that as your breathing becomes slower your mind becomes more at peace and aware.

The Second Way

The second way to consciousness is through the emotional functions. Collin asserted this is a combination of what the West calls mysticism and charity. Mysticism deals with our most basic beliefs, concepts, and attitudes. It is the belief that one can attain direct knowledge of God through subjective experiences, such as intuition or insight. Charity is generosity and helpfulness especially toward the needy or suffering. It is a demonstration of love and goodwill towards humanity. Through faith and generosity, one can change fear into love. It is the way of the monk, or nun.

The second way to consciousness is the "Spiritual Way." It holds the view that the spirit or supernatural essence is the prime element of reality. The Spiritual path requires sincerity, devotion, and the inner conviction that God alone is the true source of all peace and happiness. It is the way of faith. For those who take this path with faith, no test is too great, and obstructions become blessings.

Edgar Cayce (1877-1945) was one of America's greatest psychics, and the most documented clairvoyant of the twentieth century. People called him "the sleeping prophet" because he could put himself into some kind of self-induced sleep like state, or trance. His followers believed this state of mind enabled him to tap into some sort of higher consciousness. In addition, Cayce was a lifelong Christian. He taught Sunday school most of his life, and was an elder in his church. Regarding his spiritual insights, he stressed that we are all God's children (regardless of our religious affiliation), and that Jesus came to show us all the way back to God. In this sense, Jesus is the "pattern" for every soul on earth.

According to Cayce, spirit is the life force (an animating or vital principle that gives life to physical organisms). In addition, it is a force with consciousness and individuality. Cayce asserted, "Spirit is the spark, or portion of the Divine that is in every entity." This spark or spirit within us is our real self. This is the first stage to spiritual enlightenment - to know that we are primarily spiritual beings.

1Corinthians 2:9-16 states, "But as it is written: *Eye has not seen, nor ear heard, nor have entered into the heart of man the things which God has prepared for those who love Him. (Isaiah 64:4)'* But God has revealed them to us through His Spirit. ... No one knows the things of God except the Spirit of God. ... The natural man does not receive the things of the Spirit of God, for they are foolishness to him; nor can he know them, because they are spiritually discerned. However, he who is spiritual judges all things, yet he himself is *rightly* judged by no one. For *'who has known the mind of the LORD that he may instruct Him? (Isaiah 40:13)'* But we have the mind of Christ."

1Corinthians 2:9-16 tells us we can only understand the things of God's Spirit through spiritual discernment (When it comes to two very similar phenomena, this is how the Spirit shows us which is true and which is false). Discernment is a gift from God, although you can become better at it through training and experience. We can understand the working of God's Spirit though our spirit. Our spirit is our direct connection with God. The Holy Spirit (the third person of the Christian Trinity) leads us and teaches us through the spirit.

Proverbs 1:7 ask the question, "How does a man become wise? The first step is to trust and reverence the Lord!" Spiritual life means to be in association with God. It means having a personal walk, or intimate relationship with God, and willingly rendering devotional service to Him. When one develops a personal relationship with God as servant, one's awareness and appreciation of God is increased. This is because spirituality is a product of our submission and obedience to His Word. John 14:15 states, "If you [really] love Me, you will keep (obey) My commands."

There is a good and bad struggle in all of us. "For our struggle is not against flesh and blood, but ... against the spiritual forces of evil ... (Ephesians 6:12)" This is spiritual warfare. Therefore, you need spiritual weapons. "Therefore put on the full armor of God ... Stand firm then, with the belt of truth buckled around your waist, with the breastplate of righteousness in place, and with your feet fitted with the readiness that comes from the gospel of peace. ... In addition to all this, take up the shield of faith, with which you can extinguish all the flaming arrows of the evil one. Take the helmet of salvation and the sword of the Spirit, which is the word of God. In addition, pray in the Spirit on all occasions with all kinds of prayers and requests ... (Ephesians 6:13-18)"

From a spiritual point of view, the devil is real. He is the ultimate spirit of evil. Although created by God, he is the adversary of God. In Jewish and Christian belief, he is the ruler of hell, and the leader of all the other spirits who followed him and rebelled against God. Satan is a universal consciousness whose sole aim is to deceive us. The only way we can free ourselves is by realizing our divine nature and purpose. Our true and proper position is that of a willing servant, ready to obey God's slightest command.

Each seeker has a set of self-created delusions to overcome. To achieve this goal one must meditate on God, both day and night. Meditation is a process of cleansing the heart. It is a means of helping one to understand one's relationship with God. Through meditation on God, mental speculation and doubt will disappear. One begins to understand that God lives within one's heart always.

Meditation is a method of tuning ones mind and body to the spiritual vibrations of God. It is a necessary mental activity for a person of knowledge and power. The goal is to be intensely aware in everything we do, even our work. On the spiritual path, our work is a form of meditation. Through meditation and self-transcendence, we can break the yoke of bondage imposed on us by our egos. This is the actual meaning of the expression "Self-Realization".

When you are not meditating, you should try focusing the mind at the point between the eyebrows (the spiritual eye). This spot is the "Christ Center." It is the place to focus your concentration. Concentrating on the Christ center increases the will. This is the center of one's awareness. This point between the eyebrows is the broadcasting station in the body. Call to God from there. Then listen and feel his response in your heart, the body's receiving station.

Most people who worship have a motive; some want salvation, and others want material prosperity. However, as long as you have selfish motives, you will never be able to reach the stage of "pure love of God." Pure devotion is devoid of ambition and desire. It is rendering loving service simply for its own sake. However, do not be afraid to ask for what you want. We are Gods children, and a parent is pleased when their kids are healthy and happy.

From a spiritual point of view, the development of self-realization begins with the understanding that the true self (in essence) is pure spiritual energy. The next step is to realize that this spiritual energy is a spark from God's eternal flame. You begin to understand that you and the "Absolute Truth" are one in essence. The last step is to learn how to live fully in this transcendental relationship, so that you may dwell in the joy and wisdom of the Lord. If you want to realize your essence, you have to understand God in truth. This is the way to all true knowledge, and wisdom.

True happiness depends on attitude, not outward circumstances. With the right attitude, it is possible to recover quickly, even from great sorrow. Because people are spiritual by nature, one must attain love of God. When you feel a compelling urge to help someone without anything in return, this is the actual feel of God's perfect love. The highest love is the love of God. This means love that has nothing to do with desire, material benefit, or philosophical understanding. This consciousness is the highest perfection of human life, and is the ultimate aim of all methods of self-realization.

One achieves "God consciousness" by performing service that satisfies God, not by forming one's own way. You may think that you are doing something in God consciousness, but who has sanctioned it? For no one knows the things of God except the Spirit of God. We must then shape our desires so that they conform to God's desires. We must purify our senses, and use them for His satisfaction instead of our own. However, a person who serves God in order to satisfy God's senses becomes satisfied.

God is the supreme or ultimate reality. He is the creator and ruler of the universe, and all possible universes. He is an eternal Spirit perfect in power, wisdom, and goodness. He is an infinite consciousness, and man is a manifestation of that consciousness. The focalized consciousness in your mind that you call "I," is in reality God's consciousness. Every cell of your body has its own consciousness, which in reality is also God's consciousness. This consciousness, self or cell, is God's; and is controlled by God's will. Your will is only an iota of God's will, which he allows you to use. The use of power demonstrates an understanding of God's will, which he supplies based on your capacity to use it.

In Summary, the second way to consciousness is through the emotional functions. Through faith and generosity, one can change fear into love. This is the "Spiritual Way." It is the belief that one can attain direct knowledge of God through subjective experiences, and that the spirit or supernatural essence is the prime element of reality.

From a spiritual point of view, the devil is real. Satan is a universal consciousness whose sole aim is to deceive us. Because of this, there is a good and bad struggle in all of us. This is spiritual warfare. The only way we can free ourselves is by realizing our divine nature and purpose. Our true and proper position is that of a willing servant, ready to obey God's slightest command.

Spiritual life means having a personal walk, or intimate relationship with God. Meditation is a method of tuning ones mind and body to the spiritual vibrations of God. It is a process of cleansing the heart. It is a means of helping one to understand one's relationship with God.

The development of self-realization begins with the understanding that the true self (in essence) is pure spiritual energy. The next step is to realize that this spiritual energy is a spark from God's eternal flame. The last step is to learn how to live fully in this transcendental relationship, so that you may dwell in the joy and wisdom of the Lord. This is the way to all true knowledge, and wisdom.

Only by doing God's will can you become truly free. When you align your will with God's will, you find true freedom. The real life and work of each cell is giving up its individual life for the body as a hole. One of the keys to inner peace is the ability to accept things as they are. We have to learn to listen, to accept, and to absorb. Soul intuition, not intellect, is the real key to understanding. In addition, love, not knowledge, is the highest wisdom.

The Third Way

The third way to consciousness is through the intellectual functions (overcoming thought). It is changing thought into understanding. It is the way of philosophy. Collin asserted that in the third way one tries to think of things in terms of universal or cosmic law, and that "In this way he gradually becomes liberated from a subjective point of view and acquires objective understanding." You have to sacrifice self-deception, prejudice, and inconsistency. This will enable you to understand what you do and why. Factors that affect our thinking include:

1. Absolute objectivity is impossible. However, objectivity can be increased by being open to one's feelings; and always being concerned with knowing the truth, even though it maybe unpleasant.

2. A threat to the self-concept can be a powerful stimulus to self-deception. There is a "Psychological Ohms Law" which asserts, "The resistance to a new idea is directly proportional to the threat of the new idea to the self-concept."

3. Our personal point of view - This is the way, or how, we perceive things. It determines our values, our self-concept, and our frame of reference (a person's organized body of accumulated knowledge and experiences).

Epistemology, or the theory of knowledge, is the branch of Western philosophy that studies the nature and scope of knowledge. It is the study of knowledge, truth, science, and logic. It primarily addresses the questions: "What is knowledge?" "How is knowledge acquired?" and "What do people know?" It maintains four forms of knowledge:

1. You know by thinking (rationalism).

2. You know by observation or sensory input (empiricism).

3. You know by revelation. It is direct knowledge without thinking, from an outside supernatural source (mysticism or intuition).

4. You know by testimony (authoritarianism).

Skeptics are people disposed to skepticism. That is, they have an attitude of doubt. True skeptics assert there is no real knowledge. They fine doubt in everything. However, there are three major theories of truth:

1. "The Correspondence Theory (Empiricism)" - This theory states that a proposition, a statement, or a sentence is true when the facts correspond or accurately describes the proposition. That is, if it accurately represents the facts then it is true. Example; "The chair is green" (observation).

2. "The Pragmatic Theory (Naturalism)" - This is a product of an American philosophy called Pragmatism. It defines truth in terms of usefulness and acceptance. If you can verify it, and practically apply it, then it is true - "Try it. If it works then it's true."

3. "The Coherence Theory (Rationalism)" - This theory states that the truth is primarily a property of whole systems of propositions and gives merit to individual propositions only according to their coherence with the whole. That is, a proposition is true to the extent that it is a necessary constituent of a systematically coherent whole. "If it is logically consistent with what is known than it is true" (If $A + B = E$ and $C + D = E$ than $A + B = C + D$).

The mind is cable of functioning independently. However, our emotions usually control our thinking, and our feelings can change at any moment. Our emotions are dependent on many things, from our hunger to our surroundings. The object is to separate one's thoughts from one's feelings. However, emotions have their place. Our feelings are in direct contact with the spiritual.

Do not be afraid of your emotions. Instead, learn how to manage them.

Robert Plutchik (1928-2006) was an American psychologist, and honorary professor at the Albert Einstein College of Medicine, and adjunct professor at the University of South Florida. He developed a psycho-evolutionary theory of feeling and emotion. He proposed that the "basic" emotions are biologically primitive and have evolved for proposes of species survival. He showed how these emotions are triggers of behavior with high survival value (i.e. fear: fight-or-flight response). In 1980, he developed a scheme for classifying emotions (see Figure 3-2). He figured there are eight primary emotions- anger, fear, sadness, disgust, surprise, curiosity, acceptance and joy. The emotions labeled outside the circle describe a blend of the more basic emotions labeled inside the circle.

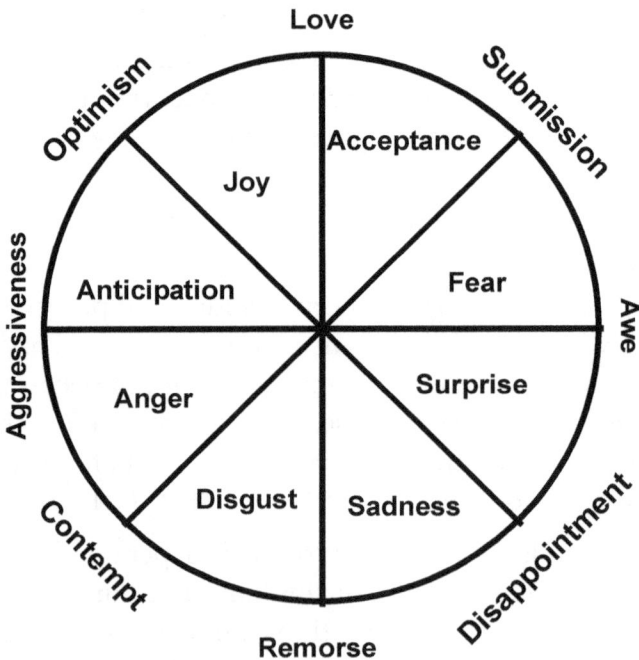

Figure 3-2: Robert Plutchik's scheme of emotions

If a person understands the difference between essence and personality; then they know what is within them, and what is outside of them. That is they know themselves and their relationship to the universe. Personality is the pattern of characteristic behaviors, thoughts, and emotions that we use to deal with our environment. It comes from the Latin word persona. It is a player's mask. It acts as a "psychological membrane," or skin, between our essence and the outside world. It has both genetic and environmental roots. Certain aspects of personality remain stable over a lifetime, while other aspects change often (because of new experiences). You can change personality through various forms of behavior modification, including hypnosis.

If personality is the light one reflects, then essence is that which one absorbs. You are it and it is you. Essence is unique. It is a combination of what you were born with, and the natural development of what you were born with. Change of essence is difficult, but possible. When one really understands something, it is absorbed into them, and becomes a part of their essence. As one continues to absorb truth and knowledge, ones essence begins to grow and change.

Through observation, you can learn what belongs to essence, and what belongs to personality. Real control is in essence, not personality. What we usually call will is only ego. Ego is the portion of our personality that think it is the self, or "I." Something say, "I like," "I want," and thinks it is will. However, "true will" dwells in essence (see Figure 2-5).

To see the world as a warrior, who is a person of knowledge and power, you have to develop the true will. Your "true will" will lead you to true liberation. Self-will is the impulses that come from the ego. It hinders you from acquiring true will. The possession of one's true will is the mark of a real person. To posse one's own "I" and "true will" is a great achievement. Even those who seek it sincerely may never attain it.

The ability to focus your attention greatly aids in the development of your true will. Psychologists, Norman and Bobrow (1975), described attention as a mental effort, or a pool of mental resources. All of our mental activities require our attention. It is the process of focusing on a few stimuli while selectively ignoring others. We tend to see what we expect to see, or what we are looking for. This phenomenon is selective perception. When we expect a particular thing to happen, we focus our attention in advance to clues that will indicate the event.

In Ouspensky's book, "In Search of the Miraculous", Gurdjieff asserted that in our ordinary reality we do not "remember ourselves;" that is, we are not aware of ourselves "at the moment" of a perception. We do not feel ourselves. We simply observe an event. When you remember yourself, you do not simply observe an event. You feel it, and there are two impressions. You get one impression of the event, and another of yourself being aware of it.

"Self-Remembering" are those frames of mind where we can experience our environment, while at the same time maintain our sense of "I." In his book "The Theory of Celestial Influence", Collin asserted self-remembering enables a person to shed the outer skin of personality. This allows them to feel and act freely from their essence. This is what it means to be "yourself."

You achieve self-remembering through the control of your attention. This is the psychological control of the molecular state of matter in the body. There are three levels or states of attention:

1. The first level is cellular (normal or passive).

2. The second level is molecular (soul or active).

3. The third level is electronic (spirit or mediator).

On the first level, a person seeing the world is fascinated. They are wholly absorbed in what they see. This is the normal state of humanity.

On the second level, you see both the world, and yourself looking at it. This is self-remembering, the practice of divided attention (the ability to remain fully focused on two or more things at the same time). By dividing your attention, you become aware of yourself, and your situation at the same time. Collin wrote, "You began to grow a soul. ... Man's soul is the totality of self-consciousness during his life time." On the third level, one sees that both ones' self and their situation stand in the presence of a higher power. This level is beyond ordinary man. Each level is a world in itself, with its own perceptions, and its' own relationship to the universe.

The "self-dialogue technique" helps you with the practice of self-remembering. This technique gives directions to your non-conscious mind. This then produces the desired effects, either in the immediate present or distant future. The self-dialogue technique requires a state of deep relaxation, combined with awareness. The object is to create a dialogue with positive mental images that will help you to reach your desired goal.

The rule is to use these instructions until you have changed your basic attitudes and behavior. These instructions are mental directives. You should give them in a positive manor, with confidence and self-assurance. You should "never" give yourself any negative commands during this process. There are four steps in the self-dialogue technique:

1. Create a dialogue with positive mental images. Picture yourself, as you want to be, than create a positive dialogue that reinforces this image.

2. Find a comfortable location and assume a relaxed position.

3. Use meditation techniques to achieve a state of deep relaxation, combined with awareness.

4. Repeat constructed dialogue in a positive manor.

Memory is the key to self-remembering. It stores our experiences. This enables us to function swiftly and automatically. Reasoning, which includes problem solving and decision-making, would be all but impossible without memory. Mark Van Doren (1894-1973) was an American born Pulitzer Prize-winning poet, editor, and critic. He earned a B.A. from the University of Illinois in 1914 and a Ph.D. from Columbia University in 1920. He wrote, "Memory performs the impossible for man. It holds together the past and the present. It gives continuity and dignity to human life. It is the companion, the tutor, the poet, and the library with which you travel."

Consciousness generates memory. If there is no consciousness, there is no memory. The idea is that mental activity transcends the physical condition. This means that mind and memory is not subject to the physical limitations of the brain. They are purely psychological phenomenon. They are a non-sensory and non-physiological function.

Your mind in realty is one. However, for the sake of clarity of communication, we will separate it into three distinct levels: conscious, subconscious, and supra conscious or intuitive mind. Conscious mind function only while you are awake. It reasons, analyzes, and control voluntary actions. It initiates recall, but remembers nothing.

Subconscious mind functions like a tape recorder. It records every impression, thought, and feeling. It also controls involuntary activity. It is the center of all habits. On an even deeper level, it contains inherited memories of the entire human race. Carl Jung called this the "Collective Unconscious." He asserted, "The unconscious is the unwritten history of mankind from time unrecorded." Therefore, memory is perfect by nature. You cannot train it, improve it, or develop it. Memory is a facet of the mind. It has an unlimited capacity to retain and recall all experiences.

Hypnosis is a temporary narrowing of conscious awareness, with an intense state of concentration. People have practiced hypnosis since ancient times, but until recently, many people regarded it as nothing more than a stage trick. However, it is in fact an important psychological tool. It can be used to alter behavior (stop smoking), and to relieve pain. There are three degrees of hypnosis:

1) Lite hypnosis, the subject becomes sleepy and follows simple directions.

2) Moderate hypnosis, the person experiences a dulling of sensory perception, similar to that of anesthesia.

3) Deep hypnosis, although the subject can talk and move around with open eyes, they could undergo medical procedures with no anesthetic.

Hypnosis and depth analysis has demonstrated we have a perfect memory. Ernest Hilgard (1904-2001) was an American psychologist who became famous in the 1950s for his research on hypnosis. He explained hypnosis in terms of the Hidden Observer Theory. He concluded that part of the unconscious mind is watching, and recording everything that is going on. However, because of the power of suggestion, some of our conscious recollections could be a mixture of fact and fantasy. Others could be false.

The supra conscious mind functions independent of ordinary thought processes. It is responsible for extrasensory perception. This is the intuitive ability to comprehend knowledge without sensory input. All creativity is an extrasensory experience, even a simple idea. Intuition is a natural function of the mind. You can achieve controlled intuition by means of deep relaxation, self-commands, and quiet listening. As you do this, creative thoughts, ideas, and revelations will come to you. There is no limit to what your supra conscious or intuitive mind will produce.

In his book "The Impersonal Life (1941)," Joseph S. Benner wrote, "To Think is to Create ... As you think in your Heart, so is it with you. ... A Thinker is a Creator who lives in a world of his own conscious creation. ... If you believe a thing is so, is not that thing really so - to you? ... If this is true, then your body, your personality, your world, is what they appear to be to you, because you have thought them into their present status." In a sense, reality is in the eyes of the beholder. Different people see things in different ways. One person's reality is another person's illusion.

In Summary, the third way to consciousness is through the intellectual functions. It is changing thought into understanding. It is the way of philosophy. Factors that affect our thinking include:

1. Absolute objectivity is impossible. However, objectivity can be increased by being open to one's feelings; and always being concerned with knowing the truth, even though it maybe unpleasant.

2. A threat to the self-concept can be a powerful stimulus to self-deception. There is a "Psychological Ohms Law" which

asserts, "The resistance to a new idea is directly proportional to the threat of the new idea to the self-concept."

3. Our personal point of view - This is the way, or how, we perceive things. It determines our values, our self-concept, and our frame of reference (a person's organized body of accumulated knowledge and experiences).

When a person begins to understand the difference between essence and personality, they start to understand themselves and their relationship to the universe. Through observation, you can learn what belongs to essence, and what belongs to personality. True will dwells in essence. To posse one's own "I" and "true will" is a great achievement. The possession of one's own "I" and "true will" is the mark of a real person. The ability to focus your attention greatly aids in the development of your true will.

"Self-Remembering" are those frames of mind where we can experience our environment, while at the same time maintain our sense of "I." You do not simply observe an event. You feel it, and there are two impressions. You get one impression of the event, and another of yourself being aware of it. Self-remembering enables a person to shed the outer skin of personality, and allows them to feel and act freely from their essence. You achieve self-remembering through the control of your attention. Self-remembering is the practice of divided attention (the ability to remain fully focused on two or more things at the same time). By dividing your attention, you become aware of yourself, and your situation at the same time. You began to grow a conscious soul.

The mind is cable of functioning independently. However, our emotions usually control our thinking, and our feelings can change at any moment. Because of this, we must learn how to manage our emotions. Robert Plutchik proposed that the 'basic' emotions are biologically primitive and have evolved for proposes of species survival. He showed how these emotions are triggers of behavior with high survival value (i.e. fear: fight-or-flight response).

You have only one mind, but it has three distinct levels: conscious, subconscious, and supra conscious or intuitive mind. Conscious mind function only while you are awake. It reasons, analyzes, and control voluntary actions. Subconscious mind controls involuntary activity, and is the center of all habits. The supra conscious mind is responsible for extrasensory perception. This is the intuitive ability to comprehend knowledge without sensory input.

The Fourth Way

The fourth way to consciousness consists of mastering the physical functions, the emotional functions, and the intellectual functions all at the same time - simultaneously. It is changing pain, fear, and thought into will, love, and understanding. This way embraces all sides of a person under ordinary conditions of life. Because of this, you do not have to be as extreme in any one function. You do not give up anything in ordinary life. You work with all three sides of yourself, your instincts, your emotions, and your intellect. This re-aligns and balances your self. You reach a state of harmony and equilibrium. There will be external results as well as internal. The results of your efforts will not only benefit you the individual, but society as a whole.

The main characteristic of the fourth way is its' harmony. In this way, the other three ways work together. If you are trying to serve God (an emotional function) by performing your work (a physical function), and at the same time you understand what you are doing and why (an intellectual function), then each reinforces the others. Collin wrote, "The man who has worked by the fourth way... has endeavored to become conscious in all his functions and in all situations... For him, consciousness will not be dependent on special associations, but will be that which accompanies him always, fasting or drinking wine, alone or in a crowd, laboring or meditating. It will be that which lights up all that happens."

These three functions: the physical, the emotional, and the intellectual work together intimately. You cannot affect one without affecting the others. This means that a certain kind of thought connects with a certain kind of emotion (or mental state), and with a certain kind of movement or physical posture. One brings about the others. Now imagine that you have decided to think in a different way. Then you see someone that you dislike, for whatever reason.

This dislike immediately arouses old thoughts and feelings. Moreover, before you know it, you find yourself thinking in the same old way.

Gurdjieff asserted, "The fourth way differs from the other ways in that the principal demand made upon a man is the demand for understanding. A man must do nothing that he does not understand, except as an experiment under the supervision and direction of his teacher. The more a man understands what he is doing, the greater will be the results of his efforts. This is a fundamental principle of the fourth way. The results of work are in proportion to the consciousness of the work. No 'faith' is required on the fourth way; on the contrary, faith of any kind is opposed to the fourth way. On the fourth way, people must satisfy themselves of the truth. You cannot simply accept what you hear. And until he is satisfied he must do nothing."

In summary, the "second task" of a person of knowledge and power is to develop their consciousness, both subjective and objective. In this way, you awaken yourself to new levels of awareness; and increase both your knowledge and power. Karl Popper proposed a "three world" theory of knowledge, which includes both subjective knowledge and objective knowledge. "World 1" is the physical world, the world of physics. "World 2" is the psychological world, the world of subjective experiences. "World 3" is the world of objective knowledge, the world of the products of the mind.

There are three traditional ways to develop your consciousness. The first way to consciousness is the ascetic way - through the instinctive and motor functions, or physical functions. You gain the ability to control yourself, through difficult physical exercises and body postures. In its full form, this is Hatha Yoga. The second way to consciousness is through the emotional functions. This is the way of faith. It is the way of the monk, or nun. The third way to consciousness is through the intellectual functions. This approach is through knowledge and understanding. It is changing thought into understanding. It is the way of the philosopher.

The fourth way to consciousness consists of mastering the physical functions, the emotional functions, and the intellectual functions all at the same time. The main characteristic of the fourth way is its' harmony. You work with all three sides of yourself, your instincts, your emotions, and your intellect. This re-aligns and balances yourself; you reach a state of harmony and equilibrium. Gurdjieff's fourth way teachings are usually classified under the "occult" headings, and stands at the crossroads of different beliefs, including Sufi traditions, Hindu and Sikh traditions, the Kabbalah, and Christian and Buddhist traditions.

Chapter Four

The Three Areas of Human Experience

The "third task" of a person of knowledge and power is to learn to interact with the world around them on a conscious level. Edmund Husserl (1859-1938) was a German philosopher, known as the father of phenomenology (the study of the development of human consciousness and self-awareness as a preface to or a part of philosophy). The "Phenomenological Ego" is the stream of consciousness in which one acquires meaning and reality from the surrounding environment. According to Husserl the phenomenological ego can become and observer of itself, and learn about it's self as we learn about the environment around us. In addition, we can only observe the results of our emotions and thoughts through the responses of other humans.

John G. Bennett (1897-1974) was a British scientist, mathematician, author, and philosopher who integrated scientific research with studies of Asiatic languages and religions. He was also a student of Gurdjieff and Ouspensky He wrote many books on psychology and spirituality. In his book, "Gurdjieff: Making a New World," he asserted there are three areas of human experience:

1. The Area of Fact - This is pre-eminently the domain in which science, technology and economics operates. This area of philosophy is naturalism, or materialism. It asserts that all existence is physical.

2. The Area of Value - This is pre-eminently the domain of morality, of aesthetics and of jurisprudences. Axiology is the

general branch of philosophy that looks at what values are, and what the good life is.

3. The Area of Realization - This is the domain of creativity, intuition, and religion. It is an area of "non-ordinary reality." This area of philosophy is idealism, or rationalism. It asserts that mind, and thoughts are most real.

The Area of Fact

The first area of human experience is "The Area of Fact." Bennett wrote, "This comprises all that is in communication with our bodies by sense perception and mechanical interaction. This is pre-eminently the domain in which science, technology and economics operates. For materialistic and mechanistic theories of the world, this is the sole reality." In philosophy, this area of reality is naturalism, or materialism. Theses theories assert that physical matter is the only or fundamental reality and that all beings, processes, and phenomena are manifestations or results of matter. They assert:

1. All existence is physical. Sensory input and physical experiences are most real.

2. Life has no supernatural significance. There is no life after death, no soul, and no God.

3. All knowledge begins with observation.

4. The physical world is a random creation.

In this area of human experience, we analyze everything from a scientific point of view. There are two major lines of science: 1) the natural sciences (as physics, chemistry, or biology), which study natural phenomena; and 2) the social sciences, which study human behavior and societies. However, in the broadest sense, science refers to any system of objective knowledge. This objective knowledge covers general truths or the operation of general laws obtained and tested through the scientific method (principles and procedures for the systematic pursuit of knowledge involving the recognition and formulation of a problem, the collection of data through observation and experiment, and the formulation and testing of hypotheses).

Science is the formal processes people use to investigate natural phenomena. These processes produce useful information and knowledge. Engineers use this knowledge to design and build tools and systems that exploit natural phenomena for practical human means. This practical application of knowledge is technology. Engineers work within the constraints of natural laws and societal needs to create new technologies.

Economics is a social science that studies the production, distribution, and consumption of goods and services. In the modern world, new technologies can spur the development of more elaborate and robust economies. This leads to a greater use of technology. (The assembly line - being able to mass produce cars lead to a greater use of automobiles). Because of its economic aspects, technology is an inseparable part of human society.

In general, governments manage the resources within their control based on their economic policies. In the United States, the laissez-faire principle (Unrestrained economic activity enforced by the state) allows the market to determine the allocation of various resources, as well as which entities gain control of them. In the socialist countries of Western Europe, governments maintain grater control over public goods and services. While in the Far East, Marxist-derivative systems assure that almost all public resources remain in control of their governments.

This area of human experience teaches us, from an early age, that our "so called" natural world is an institutionalized society. A society is a collective association with others. It may refer to a particular group of people, to a nation, or to a group of nations, such as Western society. These groups have common interest, such as religion, culture, or politics. Institutions are established organizations in a society or culture. They are ways and means to social order. They govern the behavior of their members by making and enforcing rules. Institutions include everything from churches, to big corporations, to schools, to hospitals, to governments.

We are social creatures by nature. However, it is through communication that we are able to establish meaningful connections with others. Language is our primary means of communicating.

Each language use words and methods of combining them to represent objects, activities, and ideas. This allows people to communicate about things they have never experienced. Other forms of communication include art, religion, and ritual (body language).

Avram Noam Chomsky (born December 7, 1928) is Professor Emeritus of linguistics at the Massachusetts Institute of Technology. In 1972 he wrote, "When we study human language we are approaching what some might call the 'human essence', the distinctive qualities of mind that are, as far as we know, unique to man." Language, thought, and intelligence are among our "higher mental processes," involving complex operations. Chomsky proposed that some knowledge of language must be innate, which guarantees it to us all.

It is through language that we have formed government and civilization. Governments are the formal regime for political rulemaking and enforcement. They make decisions that the rest of us must abide by. Jean-Jacques Rousseau (1712-1778) was a Swiss philosopher whose political ideas influenced the French Revolution, the development of the socialist theory, and the growth of nationalism. He asserted:

1. Civilization has corrupted human nature.

2. The "state of nature" is what life would be like without society or civilization.

3. Power alone does not make a government legitimate, nor does it improve society.

4. The life of a "noble salvage" is one without work, language, or friends.

Thomas Hobbes (1588-1679) was an English conservative and materialist philosopher. In 1651, his famous book "Leviathan" set the agenda for nearly all subsequent Western political philosophies. According to Hobbes, life in the "state of nature" is "Solitary, poor, nasty, brutish, and short." He asserted:

1. The state of nature is chaotic and bad because people are selfish and stupid.

2. People are condemned to "war of each against all."

3. The only way out is government.

Karl Heinrich Marx (1818-1883) was a very influential philosopher from Germany. He was also a political economist, and a socialist revolutionary. He is most famous for his analysis of history in terms of class struggles. He said government was an instrument of oppression. He developed a social theory called "The Theory of Economic Determinism." This is the idea that social differences and class conflicts result from economic factors. Marx asserted there are two economic classes: 1) the higher class called the "Bourgeoisie." They are the rich and the few, and 2) the lower class called the "proletariat." They are the poor and the many.

The area of fact also includes death and dying. In modern biology, death is the natural end to life. When it is time to die, the rational accepts it. For medical science as a whole, it is the enemy (bad). In the legal community, it is the ultimate or capital punishment. Most people fear death because they assume it is bad, in part because it is unknown. Some people believe death is suffering, undignified, and painful. To overcome the fear of death:

1. People fill their lives with their family and loved ones.

2. People devote their lives to social and political affairs.

3. People devote their lives to work.

Ludwig Josef Johann Wittgenstein (1889–1951) was an Austrian philosopher who contributed several "ground breaking" works to contemporary philosophy. These works included the foundations of logic, the philosophy of mathematics, the philosophy of language, and the philosophy of mind. Wittgenstein asserted death is nothing to fear because it is not an experience. You cannot experience anything if you are not alive.

Epicurus (341-270 B.C.) was an ancient Greek philosopher, and the founder of Epicureanism (a system of philosophy based upon the teachings of Epicurus). He asserted the only reason to fear death is pain, but it is not painful. It is like going to sleep, so there is no reason to fear death.

Martin Heidegger (1889-1976) was a German philosopher. He is acknowledged to be one of the most original and important philosophers of the 20th century, but also one of the most controversial. His main concern was ontology or the study of being. He argued that awareness of death is uniquely human. This sets us apart from animals. He asserted that our lives are oriented towards death. Death puts an unknown time limit on what we can accomplish in this life. It gives us a sense of urgency. This awareness helps to give shape, direction, and meaning to life.

Elisabeth Kubler-Ross (1926-2004) was a Swiss psychiatrist and author. She made significant contributions to the field of Thanatology. This is the study, or science of the experience of dying and bereavement. In her book, "On Death and Dying (1969)," she suggested that the dying person goes through "Five Stages of Grief" in dealing with their impending death. The five stages of grief, in sequential order, are denial, anger, bargaining, depression, and acceptance. Not all people experience all five stages, and some individuals may experience more than one stage at a time. Some people believe that these five stages also apply to the survivors of a loved one's death, as well.

The first stage is denial. The individual refuses to believe that they are going to die. They might insist that the doctors are wrong. However, this attitude usually changes before death. The second stage is anger. People usually asks, "Why me?" At this point, they may take their anger and frustration out on others. In addition, they may envy the health of others. The third stage is bargaining. The person tries to delay their death. They make all types of promises to themselves and to God, in the hope that it will extend their life just a little longer.

The fourth stage is depression. It usually comes, as the end gets closer. There comes an overwhelming sense of loss. There is a loss of one's self and their relationships. In addition, there is a loss of ones will and desire. The final stage is acceptance. With the help of family, friends, and medical personnel, one finally accepts their fate. Having worked through the other stages, the dying patient can now come to their end in peace.

Many people have craved immortality. Some have proposed philosophical arguments in favor of life after death. Plato's argument for immortality assumed that souls are "absolutely" simple, and thus do not decompose. He asserted the soul is not physical. Therefore, there is no reason to believe it dies.

Immanuel Kant (1724-1804) was a German philosopher. He was one of the most influential thinkers of modern Europe. His argument for immortality was human moral experience. He asserted:

1. Our conscious demands us to be perfect.

2. Our conscious is innate, like our natural drive for sex, and a desire to stop our hunger.

3. Because we have a drive to be perfect, it must be possible to become perfect.

4. In order to reach perfection, there must be life after death, because it will take more then one lifetime to become perfect.

The fact that many people have craved immortality neither proves nor disproves the belief in life after death. However, regardless of when or why we die, there is nothing in life more certain than death. It is a reality that each of us must face. "But now, by dying to what once bound us, we have been released from the law so that we serve in the new way of the Spirit, and not in the old way of the written code. (Romans 7:6)"

In Summary, the first area of human experience is "The Area of Fact." This area of reality is naturalism, or materialism. It asserts all existence is physical; and that there is no life after death, no soul, and no God. This is the domain of science, technology and economics. Science is the formal processes people use to investigate natural phenomena. Engineers use knowledge produced by the scientific method to create new technologies. These new technologies spur the development of more elaborate and robust economies. Because of its economic aspects, technology is an inseparable part of human society.

In this area of human experience, the world is an institutionalized society. These organizations are ways and means to social order. They govern the behavior of people by making and enforcing rules. Institutions include everything from churches, to big corporations, to schools, to hospitals, to governments - which are the ultimate formal regime for rulemaking and enforcement.

The area of fact also includes death and dying. Elisabeth Kubler-Ross suggested that the dying person goes through "Five Stages of Grief" in dealing with their impending death. The five stages of grief are denial, anger, bargaining, depression, and acceptance. Having worked through the other stages, the dying patient can now come to their end in peace.

The Area of Value

The second area of human experience is "The Area of Value." Bennett wrote, "This includes all those intangible influences that determine our judgments and our motives. This is pre-eminently the domain of morality, of aesthetics and of jurisprudences. Its content is all that ought to be. Usually 'values' are regarded as ideas or attitudes held by human beings. We should treat them as having their own reality, independent of our experience. The domain of value is the 'ideal world', and for the idealist who regards mere fact as illusion, the domain of values is the 'real' world."

Axiology is the study of the nature and types of values, and of value judgments especially in ethics. It is the general branch of philosophy, which looks at what values are, and what the good life is. It looks at what makes things beautiful, and what our political rights and duties are. It includes ethics and aesthetics. Ethics deals with what is right and wrong in human conduct, and why this is the case. Aesthetics deals with artistic and expressive values.

Objectivists assert that values are the factual quality of things (The book is accurate). Value is something we find or discover in things, people, or situations themselves. It is a quality of the object, not the person, or persons viewing it. On the other hand, subjectivists assert that value judgments describe people's attitude towards things (I like this book). Value judgments, attitudes, and opinions of people are the main thing. The value is not in the objects themselves.

Friedrich Wilhelm Nietzsche (1844-1900) was an existentialist philosopher from Germany. He produced critiques of religion, morality, contemporary culture, and philosophy. He asserted that there are two sources of morality: The "Slave

Morality", and the "Master Morality." The slave morality comes from the lower class of people. Their values include charity, equality, and brotherly love. Their main aim is to be free from pain. The master morality comes from the higher class of people. Their values include self-mastery, self-discipline, independence, and nobility. They make up their own values. They seek-out challenges and self-fulfillment. Nietzsche thought that the slaves are in control, and that it is hurting the masters (the over man, or superman). He also asserted:

1. Power is the only thing in life that has value.

2. The basic force behind power is will and desire, and that we should develop as many of our abilities as possible.

3. The object is to live our lives such that we would want everything in our lives to happen again.

Joseph Fletcher (1905-1991) was an American professor and Episcopalian priest. He founded the theory of Situation Ethics in 1960, and was a pioneer in the field of bioethics. In his book, "Situation Ethics: The New Morality," he asserted that love alone is always good and right, regardless of the situation. However, he later renounced his belief in God and became an atheist.

Bertrand Russel (1872-1970) was A British philosopher, logician (a subfield of mathematics), and mathematician. In 1950, he became a Nobel Laureate in Literature. He was for clear speaking and thinking. He thought ethics was propaganda. It is trying to get someone to accept your values, including: 1) Making laws and enforcing them, and 2) Preaching - trying to get others to accept your views through words.

Kant said we are not accountable for our actions because we cannot predict the consequences. He asserted: 1) the motive, a sense of duty, is important. Duties are always right. They are what you wish everyone would do, and 2) "The Categorical Imperative" - The morality of an action comes from the rule behind it. An action is right only if it is what everyone should do (a universal law).

The area of value also includes work, play, and art. Work is expanding energy, making an effort. It used to be "try to relax in the world," then along came "America's Work Ethic." Nietzsche called it the vice of the New World. It emphasized the personal and social importance of work. It has origins in both religious and secular values. Its religious origin comes from the "Protestant Work Ethic." It asserts: 1) Work is good. In fact, it is our duty to work. Because of this, we should do our best, and 2) it is God's will for us to have a vocation.

The secular origin of America's work ethic was a result of pioneer life. People had to work hard just to stay alive. It was a fact of their environment. In addition, it was the only way to improve their standard of living. Each generation could contribute something to the next. Some people called this the "Spirit of Capitalism."

Karl Marx's "Theory of Alienation" asserted that if you feel like a stranger while you are working, it is because you are alienated from three things:

1. You are alienated from yourself. Marks said we live to work. The workers can only support themselves by working. He thought this was bad because you are only yourself when you are not working.

2. You are alienated from the product. The artisan creates something, and it is theirs, but most workers are alienated from their products. Because what they make, they do not get to keep.

3. You are alienated from others. The ideal is that we can relate to each other for the common outcome. However, this cannot happen in capitalism because of the competition (Someone is trying to get your job).

One of the most prevalent images of humanity today is the phrase "Homo Faber." This literally means, "Man the Maker or Worker." It refers to humans as controlling the environment through tools. Other characteristics of "Homo Faber" include:

1. People are toolmakers and users, including science and ideas (technology).

2. People destroy nature by cutting trees, by removing elements from the soil, and by releasing chemicals into the atmosphere.

3. People continue to work even when there is no need (workaholics).

4. People make themselves. They create their own identities through vocation.

In anthropology, "Homo Faber" confronts "Homo Ludens." The term "Homo Ludens" literally means, "Man as Player." It refers to humans at play, and looks at life as playing - amusements, humor, and leisure. Epicurus said the good life is a tranquil mind (free of fear), and happy body (absent of pain) with long-range pleasures. In addition, some of the best pleasures are intellectual rather than physical.

Play is a form of activity. It can be necessary for kids and adults. It can be a form of relaxation, or it can be exercise. For people who take play seriously (professional athletes), play is the real world. While those who take work seriously, see play as fun or fantasy. Characteristics of play and games include:

1. Play is spontaneous, voluntary-free, and gratuitous.

2. Play is valued for its own sake, simply for the fun or joy of playing.

3. Play produces a sphere of illusion, an imaginary but involving realm.

Aesthetics comes from the Greek word aesthesis. It is a branch of philosophy dealing with sensory perceptions, and the nature of beauty, art, and taste. When enjoying such an experience, the appreciative person's attitude towards the work of art is disinterested. This means you forget your own personal interest or concern. These experiences are important because they allow people to express themselves through music, dance, and art. People like it for itself, rather then for its usefulness.

Suzanne Langer (1895-1985) was an American philosopher of art. She is famous for her 1942 book "Philosophy in a New Key." She studied art and aesthetics. She defined art as the creation of perceptible forms. These forms are expressive of human feelings. They conceptualize the inner life. In addition, it helps us to share and understand our feelings. Her primary focus was to establish a sound and systematic basis for an understanding of art - including the reasons behind its creation, and its value for human consciousness.

Leo Tolstoy (1828-1910) was a Russian novelist and moral philosopher. He was one of the greatest of all novelists, including his book "War and Peace." As a moral philosopher, he is notable for his ideas on nonviolent resistance through his work "The Kingdom of God is Within You," which in turn influenced such twentieth-century figures as Mahatma Gandhi and Martin Luther King, Jr. - Mahatma Gandhi (1869-1948) was a major political and spiritual leader of the Indian independence movement. He practiced non-violence resistance through mass civil disobedience. Martin Luther King, Jr. (1929-1968) was the most famous leader of the American civil rights movement, and considered a peacemaker throughout the world for his promotion of nonviolence and equal treatment for different races; he received the Nobel Peace Prize in 1968.

Tolstoy asserted art is an emotionally expressive form of communication. The purpose of art is to share feelings. It is good art if it communicates the feelings of the artist to a viewer. During the Stone Age, art gave man a kind of power over the animals they hunted. The idea of art was magic to them. The history of art is a history of thought and visual memory. The artist has a drive to express themselves, and a need to understand themselves and others.

In summary, the second area of human experience is "The Area of Value." This is the domain of morality, of aesthetics and jurisprudences. Axiology is the general branch of philosophy, which looks at what values are, and what the good life is. This includes ethics and aesthetics.

Nietzsche asserted that there are two sources of morality: The "Slave Morality", and the "Master Morality." The slave morality includes charity, equality, and brotherly love. Their main aim (people with a slave morality) is to be free from pain. The master morality includes self-mastery, self-discipline, independence, and nobility. They (people with a master morality) make up their own values. They seek-out challenges and self-fulfillment.

The area of value also includes work, play, and art. One of the most prevalent images of humanity today is the phrase "Homo Faber." This literally means, "Man the Maker or Worker." It refers to humans as controlling the environment through tools. The term "Homo Ludens" literally means, "Man as Player." It refers to humans at play, and looks at life as playing - amusements, humor and leisure. Art is the creation of perceptible forms, which are expressive of human feelings. They conceptualize our inner feelings, and help us to share and understand our feelings.

The person who believes that everyone in all circumstances should tell the truth to the best of their ability and never knowingly lie is an "Ethical Absolutist" (universal right and wrong). On the other hand, a "Relativist" would say nothing is universally right or wrong. It is not what you do, but why you do it. "Table 4-1" is an illustration of the development of moral reasoning as postulated by Lawrence Kohlberg (1927-1987). He was an American psychologist famous for his work in moral education, reasoning, and development.

Table 4-1:

Kohlberg's concept of the development of moral reasoning

Stage 1: Orientation to obedience and punishment **Stage 2:** Orientation to one's own pragmatic goals	**Pre-conventional Level** Morality depends on what one has to gain or lose personally
Stage 3: orientation to social approval **Stage 4:** Orientation to established social and legal order	**Conventional Level** Morality is equated with social convictions - what is approved by others or by the rules of law
Stage 5: Orientation to reciprocal rights and responsibilities **Stage 6:** Orientation to ethical principles that transcend the authority of law	**Post-conventional Level** Morality is tied to ultimate ethical principles

The Area of Realization

The third area of human experience is "The Area of Realization." Bennett wrote, "The notion of a non-factual domain in which reality is constantly being created is foreign to ordinary thinking, but it is implicit in all Gurdjieff taught and did. It is indeed the central concept of all 'work', which by definition, proceeds exclusively by creative activity that cannot be reduced to fact and value, or even a combination or the two. ... We have sense experiences and we have emotional impulses from which we construct in our minds, pictures of the world and we take these pictures for representations of reality. ... Real men are those who can create their own 'reality', but this takes them into a domain that is incomprehensible for those who believe in facts and values as 'real' in themselves."

In philosophy, this area of human experience includes idealism and rationalism. Idealism asserts that the essential nature of reality lies in consciousness or reason; and that mind, and thoughts are most real. You know by thinking. Valid knowledge begins with the clearest and most seemingly certain ideals that we have. "I think therefore I am." Rationalism asserts that reason is the basis for the establishment of religious truth; and that reason is in itself a source of knowledge superior to and independent of sense perceptions.

The area of realization is the domain of creativity, intuition, and religion. Creativity is the ability or power to create. It means to bring into existence, or to produce through imaginative skill. Intuition is the quick insight, or immediate apprehension of knowledge without rational thought. Religion is a personal set, or institutionalized system of religious attitudes, beliefs, and practices. It is the service and worship of God or the supernatural. The area of realization is an area of "non-ordinary reality." Here we can learn without direct experience. Here things can appear out of nowhere. An idea, or the answer to a question, may just come to us.

Primarily religion means to love God. It is a way of life, and a body of beliefs around a single deity (God). It is a relationship with a supernatural being. It is holy, secret, and unquestionable. It is a commitment to something special and ultimate, and promises salvation. Through ones relationship with God, reality can change. The facts may not seem possible. "Then Joshua spoke to the Lord on the day when the Lord gave the Amorites over to the Israelites, and he said in the sight of Israel, Sun, be silent and stand still at Gibeon, and you, moon, in the Valley of Ajalon! ... And the sun stood still, and the moon stayed, until the nation took vengeance upon their enemies. ... So the sun stood still in the midst of the heavens and did not hasten to go down for about a whole day. (Joshua 10: 12-13)"

Religion is not just a system of beliefs, or a formalized effort to get pity from God. True religion consists of a growing awareness of our spiritual relationship with God. "Like an addiction, religion demands that we take an active part with the hold. You have to live your religion, or it is not yours." Some of the different ways to religion include:

1. Scientific study of religion - It deals with the facts. One may or may not be a believer.

2. Theology - This is an attempt to understand and define one's belief. She is a believer.

3. Philosophy of religion - This is an attempt to rationalize religion. It questions nature and the existence of God, the soul, and life after death. It also asks is faith knowledge, and assumes the attitude of a non-believer.

Theism is belief in one or more personal gods. There are many forms of Theism, including:

1. Monotheism - There is only one God.

2. Henotheism - Many gods exist, but one is most important.

3. Deism - There are one or more impersonal gods. Deist assert that god is so removed from creation that he becomes a kind

of impersonal principle simply watching over things as they go along on their own.

4. Polytheism - Many gods exist.

5. Pantheism - God is everywhere.

6. Animism - Many impersonal spirits inhabit the world.

7. Atheism - God does not exist.

8. Agnosticism - This assert God may or may not exist. It does not know.

9. Humanism - If anything, human beings are divine.

Those forms of religion that lie in the tradition of immanence tend to see the divine as one with nature, or in the world. While those forms that lie in the tradition of transcendence, tend to see the divine as above, or beyond the ordinary world. The Judeo-Christian religious tradition has fostered a perspective that sets people apart from nature. They include in their perspective:

1. Humans are strangers in the natural world. Their true home is elsewhere.

2. Humans are more important than the rest of nature, or the universe.

3. Humans are unique creatures because they possess rational souls.

4. This world is not divine.

William James (1842-1910) was a pioneering American psychologist and philosopher. He wrote influential books on (at the time) the young science of psychology; including educational psychology, the psychology of religious experiences, and the philosophy of pragmatism. He looked toward consequences (what are the results). He asserted nether science or philosophy could prove religion. Either you are, or you are not religious. You have to believe. He asserted God is real because he has real effects on people, and that faith is a genuine option. One chooses with will rather then by intellect. He thought that religion was a good bet, "If you're wrong you don't lose much."

Nietzsche asserted, "God is dead," and that "The Aim is lacking." God is a symbol, or idea, that no longer helps us. For Nietzsche, the death of God was a way of denying a belief in cosmic or physical order, and that this will lead to a rejection of absolute values themselves. "The Death of God" for him meant:

1. We must create our own values and meanings.

2. We are free to realize our full potentials by our selves.

3. We can affirm life, rather than negate it.

The "Argument from Design," or the "Teleological Argument," is an argument for the existence of God or a creator based on perceived evidence of order, purpose, and design in nature (where there is order someone created it). Critics of the "Argument from Design" assert that:

1. If someone created the world, then it can be uncreated.

2. The argument does not prove that there is only one God.

3. The disorder and suffering in the world suggest that the design is imperfect.

Soren Kierkegaard (1813-1855) was a Danish philosopher and theologian, generally recognized as the first existentialist philosopher. Much of his work was in Christian existentialism and existential psychology. He interpreted religion as involving a leap of faith. This is the act of believing in something without, or in spite of, the objective facts. He felt that a leap of faith was necessary in order to accept Christianity because of the paradoxes that exist in Christianity. One example of this is the fact that Jesus existed as both 100% God and 100% man. Since neither logic nor reason can reconcile this, one must have faith that it is true in light of the paradox.

Kierkegaard thought that the senses have three stages, the aesthetic stage (this involves a sense of pleasure), the ethical stage (this deals with principles and commitments), and the religious stage (this involves a leap of faith). He also asserted that:

1. People are taking Christianity for granted.

2. Truth is Subjective - facts and reasons are not enough.

3. God became man in Jesus Christ.

4. God is unknown, immortal, and all knowing.

5. God and men are two different realities.

6. Religion is a matter of trust, not facts, because there is no way to prove, or disprove God with science.

In summary, the third area of human experience is "The Area of Realization." This area of philosophy is idealism, or rationalism. It asserts that the ultimate reality lies in a realm transcending natural phenomena; and that mind, and thoughts are most real. This area of human experience is an area of "non-ordinary reality." Here we can learn without direct experience. Here things can appear out of nowhere. An idea, or the answer to a question, may just come to us.

This area of realization is the domain of creativity, intuition, and religion. Creativity is the ability or power to create. It means to bring into existence, or to produce through imaginative skill. Intuition is the quick insight, or immediate apprehension of knowledge without rational thought. Religion is a personal set or institutionalized system of religious attitudes, beliefs, and practices. It is the service and worship of God, or the supernatural.

Rationalism asserts that reason is the basis for the establishment of religious truth. However, William James asserted nether science or philosophy could prove religion. Either you are, or you are not religious. You have to believe.

The area of realization is a non-factual domain. The facts may not always add up. Mind and spirit is over matter. In this area, reality can change. Here, faith is a reality. "So then faith comes by hearing, and hearing by the word of God" (Romans 10:17). True faith without experience is not possible. Reason by itself is not enough. Only the love of God can awaken true faith in his word. The deeper your awareness or experience of Gods love; the deeper your faith is. To those who can hear and understand, this area of realization is more then blind faith. It is a source of joy, power, and wisdom.

The "third task" of a person of knowledge and power is to learn to interact with the world around them on a conscious level.

Edmund Husserl asserted, the Phenomenological Ego can become an observer of it's self and learn about it's self as it learns about its environment. The question then becomes, "In what ways can we relate to our environment?"

According to Bennett, there are "Three Areas of Human Experience," which are distinguishable. The first area is "The Area of Fact." This is pre-eminently the domain in which science, technology and economics operates. This area of philosophy is naturalism, or materialism. It asserts that all existence is physical. This area of human experience gives us an objective base, with objective methods. It has enabled us to develop medicine and technology. However, it has also allowed the development of weapons of mass destruction.

The second area of human experience is "The Area of Value." This is pre-eminently the domain of morality, of aesthetics, and of jurisprudences. Its content is all that ought to be. Nietzsche asserted that there are two sources of morality: The "Slave Morality", and the "Master Morality." The slave morality values include charity, equality, and brotherly love. The master morality values include self-mastery, self-discipline, independence, and nobility. They make up their own values.

The area of value also includes work, play, and art. There are two prevailing images of humanity today. One is "Homo Faber," which literally means, "Man the Maker or Worker." It refers to humans as controlling the environment through tools. The other prevailing image is "Homo Ludens," which literally means, "Man as Player." It refers to humans at play, and looks at life as playing, amusements, or humor and leisure. Art is an act of creation. It stimulates our thoughts and emotions. It can elevate our interpretation of the world and of ourselves. Artistic works have existed since early pre-historic art.

The third area of human experience is "The Area of Realization." This is the domain of creativity, intuition, and religion. It is an area of "non-ordinary reality." This area of philosophy is idealism, or rationalism. It asserts that mind, and thoughts are most real. Rationalism asserts that reason is the basis for the establishment of religious truth; and that reason is in itself a source of knowledge superior to, and independent of sense perceptions. Religion is a way of life, and a body of beliefs, usually around a single deity, or God. True religion consists of a growing awareness of our spiritual relationship with God. Through ones relationship with God, reality can change. Here, faith is a reality.

Chapter Five

Cosmology and
Cosmological Convictions

The "fourth task" of a person of knowledge and power is to learn to see them self, and the world around them from a universal or cosmological point of view. Human beings have a threefold nature of body, soul, and spirit. Therefore, a true cosmological point of view will allow us to satisfy our threefold nature of body, soul, and spirit (regardless of our religion). Bennett wrote, "The effect is to present one with a threefold value system involving:

1. Man's concern with his own welfare in the light of his own mortality.

2. Man's place in nature and the obligations this entails.

3. Man's supernatural obligation to fulfill the purpose for which he exists."

Cosmology is the study of the universe in its totality. It deals with the nature of the universe. It tries to understand the universe as a unified whole. This includes the origin, the structure, and the space-time relationship of the universe. The study of the universe has a long history involving science, philosophy, and religion. Although the aim, methodology, and perspectives may differ, there are parallels between modern science, philosophy, and religion. This is because the same laws, which created the universe, created human beings.

In modern science, "scientific cosmology" is the branch of physics and astrophysics that deals with the study of the physical origins of the universe and the nature of the universe on its largest scale. In modern industrial societies, science seeks to explain the universe through astronomy and mathematics. Although before the

19th century, the word "science" simply meant knowledge. Science was a form of natural philosophy. Natural philosophy became science when the inductive methods of knowledge acquisition (the scientific method), became emphasized over pure deduction.

Stephen William Hawking was born in Oxford, England on January 8, 1942. He is a theoretical physicist, and the Lucasian Professor of Mathematics at the University of Cambridge, in England. He has made significant contributions to the field of quantum physics, particularly his theories regarding theoretical cosmology, quantum gravity, and black holes. In November 2001, He published a book called, "The Universe in a Nutshell." He attempted to answer questions like "Where do we come from? How did the universe begin? Did 'time' exist before the big bang? What caused the big bang? Why is the universe the way it is? How will it end?"

Hawking was attempting to uncover the elusive Theory of Everything (one complete unified theory that will describe everything that happens in the universe or cosmos). It is a hypothetical theory of theoretical physics that fully explains and links together all known physical phenomena. There have been numerous theories of everything proposed by theoretical physicists over the last century; including Albert Einstein (1879-1955). Einstein was born to a Jewish family in Germany, and considered one of the greatest physicists of all time. He believed that the only task left was to unify general relativity and electromagnetism.

The leading "theory of everything" is the String theory. It is a model in theoretical physics whose building blocks (sub-atomic particles like electrons) are one-dimensional objects (strings) rather than the zero-dimensional points (particles), which is the basis of the standard model of particle physics. These strings, which vibrate at specific resonant frequencies, are as tiny vibrating objects, opposed to points. This mean they can be in more then one place at the same time.

These objects vibrate in different modes (just as a guitar string can produce different notes), with every mode appearing as a different particle (such as electrons, protons, and neutrons).

Moreover, string theory appears to be able to "unify" the known natural forces of gravity and electromagnetism by describing them with the same set of equations. Because of the tremendous difficulty in producing experimentally testable results, no experimental verification or falsification of the theory has yet been possible.

Studies of string theory have shown that it predicts higher-dimensional objects called branes. That is, a 0-brane is a zero-dimensional particle, a 1-brane is a string, a 2-brane is a "membrane", etc. String theory strongly suggests the existence of ten or eleven space-time dimensions, as opposed to the four standard dimensions of space and time. It suggests there are an infinite number of parallel universes or membranes, each with different laws of physics. This means the "Big Bang" was nothing special, there maybe many "Big Bangs."

"Philosophical cosmology" deals with the universe in terms of the totality of space, time, and all phenomena. It uses philosophy and metaphysics to address questions about the universe that are beyond the scope of science. Historically speaking, its roots are in religion. What distinguishes it from "religious cosmology" is its approach to these questions using philosophical methods? Modern "metaphysical cosmology" tries to address questions like, "What is the origin of the universe? What is its first cause? Is its existence necessary?"

A "religious cosmology" is a system of beliefs that attempts to describe or explain the origin and structure of the universe, which includes human life. It attempts to explain the relationship between human beings and the rest of the universe. In many cases, these explanations came from scriptural teachings; but in some cases, they came through philosophical arguments. In most major religious cosmologies, God created the universe.

"Esoteric cosmology" includes many of the same concerns addressed by religious cosmology and philosophical cosmology. This cosmology attempts to integrates the spiritual with the psychological; however, its emphasis is on intellectual understanding rather than faith. Examples of esoteric cosmology include the

Kabbalah, Sufism, Gurdjieff's "Fourth Way," and some "New Age" teachings.

In Gurdjieff's system of cosmology, within the Absolute, there are three fundamental forces or laws. These three forces or laws constitute one whole, one consciousness, or one will. The interaction between these three fundamental forces is the cause of all creation. They separate and unite by their own Divine will, and create all phenomena. Collin wrote, "All we can say with truth is that the Absolute is 'One,' and that within this one, three forces, differentiating themselves as radiation, attraction and time, between them create Infinity."

In many ancient systems of philosophy, three forces created everything. These forces are active or creative, passive or material, and mediation or formative. These modifications to the Absolute represent "The Law of Three." In Christianity, they appear as the Trinity - the Father, the Son, and the Holy Ghost. In China, they appear as Yin and Yang, over seen by the Tao. These three forces are everywhere, and in everything. On the atomic level, they are electron, proton, and neutron. On the level of chemical processes, they are reactant, reagent, and catalyst. All possible colors come from the combination of blue (active), red (passive), and green or yellow (mediator).

The next concept in Gurdjieff's system of cosmology is the "The Law of Seven," or "Law of Octaves." The notes on a musical scale express the law of octaves in the form of music. The seven notes: do, re, mi, fa, sol, la, si, do form an octave; with the eighth note having a frequency twice that of the first. This represents the relationship between phenomena at all levels of existence from the atom to the universe.

Collin wrote, "We have, in fact, found the archetypal pattern for the development of all progressions. Every sequence in time or density - whether the audible notes of musical scales, the visible colors of the spectrum, or the tangible growth of organic forms - follows this octave ratio. ... All progressions and processes on earth, brought into being by the triple forces of creation, continue and proceed under this law of successive influences (the law of octaves)." This octave ratio is a language in itself. In terms of music, all can understand it. It is the mathematics of emotion. It is a form of power in itself.

The combination of the law of three and the law of seven is the archetypal pattern for Gurdjieff's doctrine of cosmoses. These are individualized states of existence with the same cosmic model, although they may differ in size and function. A cosmos is a world in itself. It is orderly, harmonious, and systematic. This brings us to a symbol Gurdjieff called "The Enneagram" (see Figure 5-1). It represents three independent processes, each interacting and supporting each other. It is a triple symbol: a triangle and hexagon inscribed within a circle. The points of the hexagon connect in such a way that the lines of the hexagon cross three times. It shows the cosmic relationship betweens grater and lesser cosmoses.

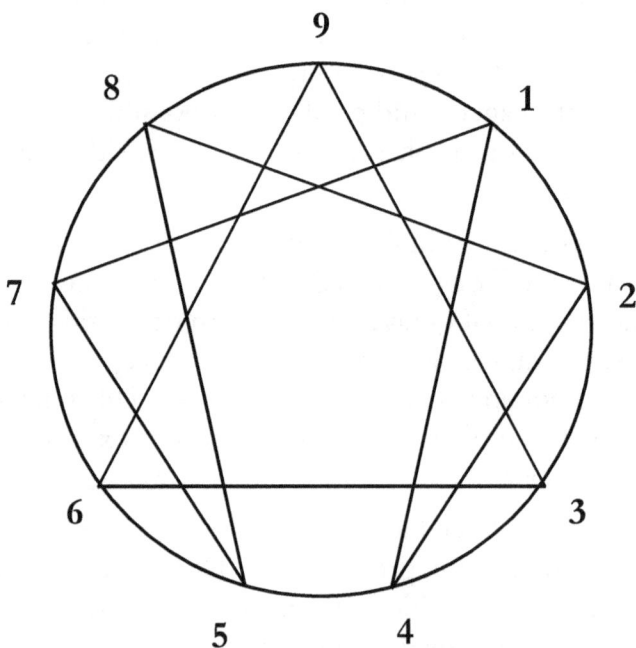

Figure 5-1: The Enneagram

There are many possible interpretation of this symbol. One interpretation is the mystical properties of the number 3 and the number 7. By numbering the points on the circumference from 1-to-9, the triangle connects the numbers 3, 6 and 9; and the hexagon connects the number 1, to 4, to 2, to 8, to 5, to 7, and back to 1. The triangle numbers are multiples of three, and one divided by three, yields an infinite sequence of threes. One divided by seven, yields an infinite repetition of the sequence 1, 4, 2, 8, 5, and 7. They are the numbers of the hexagon. These mathematical enigmas are two of the fundamental laws of the universe.

There are six processes in a cosmos. Collin wrote, "The principle that six cosmic processes, universally applicable, must result from the interaction of three forces was full recognized by 17th century alchemy, whose theory and practice was based on the six alchemical operations - coagulation, dissolution, sublimation, putrefaction, separation and transmutation - resulting from different reactions of salt, sulfur and mercury."

The six processes in a cosmos are:

1. Growth and Multiplication - This process starts immediately after conception, and continues until death. The life force enters matter and produces a living creature. The embryo becomes an infant, which becomes a child, which becomes a man. As we age, the growth process slows down and the decay process increases. This happens unconsciously and involuntarily.

2. Digestion and Decay - This is the process of purification and refinement. It is the production of nutrients from the refinement of food, water, and air. The product of one stage becomes raw material for the next. This process is complementary to the process of growth and multiplication.

3. Elimination - This is the process to exclude waste, which becomes food for some other system. This process is necessary in order to maintain a healthy and efficient state of being.

4. Corruption or Disease - This is the improper functioning of various parts of an organism. It is the failure of the process

of elimination. It represents a form of self-perpetuating crime, which will spread to other raw materials.

5. Healing - This is the process to restore health. It is the antidote to the process of corruption. There is the natural physiological healing in the body or cosmos, supported by a higher function. In the case of humanity, it is medical science and "Faith-Healing."

6. Regeneration or Re-creation - On the cosmic level the creature emulates the creator, and creates. It is the act of conception. This is the life force producing a living creature. On a universal scale, it creates the whole sequence of cosmoses.

A cosmos is a current center or transformer. It transforms energy for the purpose of "Reciprocal Maintenance." Gurdjieff asserted, "In all probability, there exists in the world some law of the reciprocal maintenance of everything existing." Bennett wrote, "Reciprocal maintenance in its special sense connotes that the universe has a built-in structure or pattern whereby every class of existing things produces energies or substances that are required for maintaining the existence of other classes." One of the keys to reciprocal maintenance is in what Gurdjieff called the "Symbol of All Life" (see Figure 5-2).

Angelic Essence   Cosmic Individual

Man

Animal   Germ

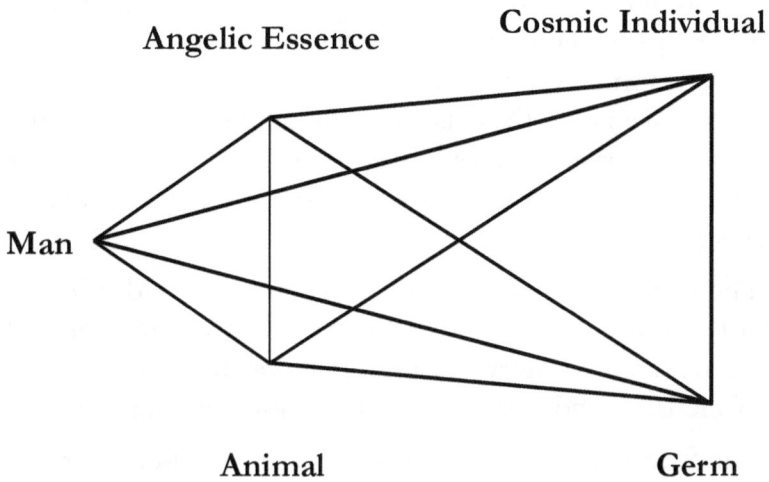

Figure 5-2: Gurdjieff's Symbol of All Life

In this symbol, each essence class has three characteristics:

1. It is what it is, and stands at the heart of its own five-term system.

2. It has limits set by the essence class above and below it.

3. It maintains other essence classes outside of its own existence.

Human beings are between the angelic essence and the animal essence. You can strive to be noble or live simply for self-gratification. However, the duality of self will not allow you to yield to either extreme. True human essence is having learned how to balance one's self.

Each individual human being is a cosmos, or center for the transformation of energy for the purpose of reciprocal maintenance. We have the principle that all cosmoses have the same basic pattern. This pattern is the combination of the cosmic laws of three and seven. When we apply these laws to human beings, we see the human body consists of seven or eight major endocrine glands that secrete hormones (see Figure 5-3). These functions are subject to three controls:

1. The Cerebrospinal: This refers to the brain and spinal cord, or to these together with the cranial and spinal nerves that innervate voluntary muscles. It serves the conscious functions, and is the seat of conscious mental processes.

2. The Sympathetic: This refers to the sympathetic nervous system (the part of the autonomic nervous system that activates the fight or flight response.). It stimulates unconscious, involuntary, or instinctive functions.

3. The Parasympathetic and Vagus: They refer to parasympathetic nervous system (the part of the autonomic nervous system that conserves energy as it slows the heart rate, increases intestinal and gland activity, and relaxes sphincter muscles in the gastrointestinal tract). They complement the sympathetic, and serve the supra conscious.

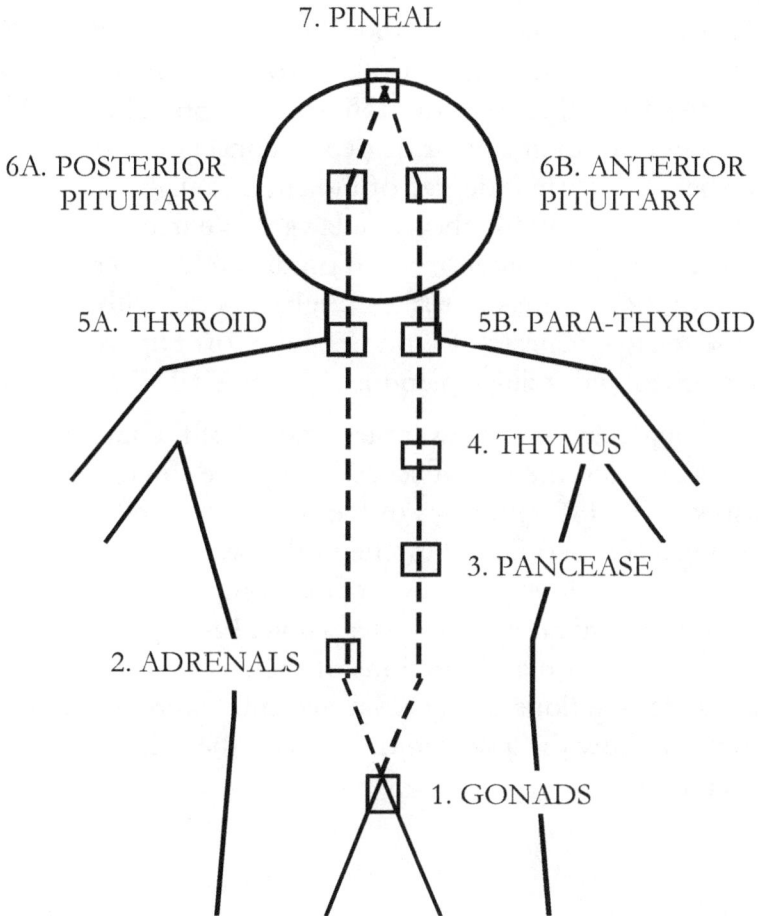

7. PINEAL

6A. POSTERIOR PITUITARY

6B. ANTERIOR PITUITARY

5A. THYROID

5B. PARA-THYROID

4. THYMUS

3. PANCEASE

2. ADRENALS

1. GONADS

Figure 5-3: The major endocrine glands

The endocrine system and its products represent the law of octaves. The three nervous controls represent the law of three. The interactions of these two laws form a living cosmos. This "Divine Image" is the "hallmark of a Cosmos." Genesis 1: 26 tell us, "God created man in his own image." Collin wrote, "All men are similar in their pattern and their constitution: so most probably are all suns. What distinguishes men is their degree of consciousness: what distinguishes suns is their degree of radiance. ... light and consciousness obey exactly the same laws ... We may even say that they are the same phenomenon, seen on different scales." "... For as we cannot look at the sun for it's brightness ... neither can we gaze at the terrible majesty of God breaking forth upon from heaven, clothed in dazzling splendor ... (Job 37: 21-22)"

A living cosmos is the simplest model of the interaction of the law of three and the law of seven. The three forces and the seven aspects are different ways of looking at the same phenomenon. If we could comprehend the law of three and the law of octaves simultaneously, then we could comprehend the solar system and the human organism as a whole. Just as digestion, respiration, and reason are functions of the cosmos of humankind; the planets are functions of the Solar System. Figure 5-3, Figure 5-4, and Table 5-1 show the association between the solar system and the human body.

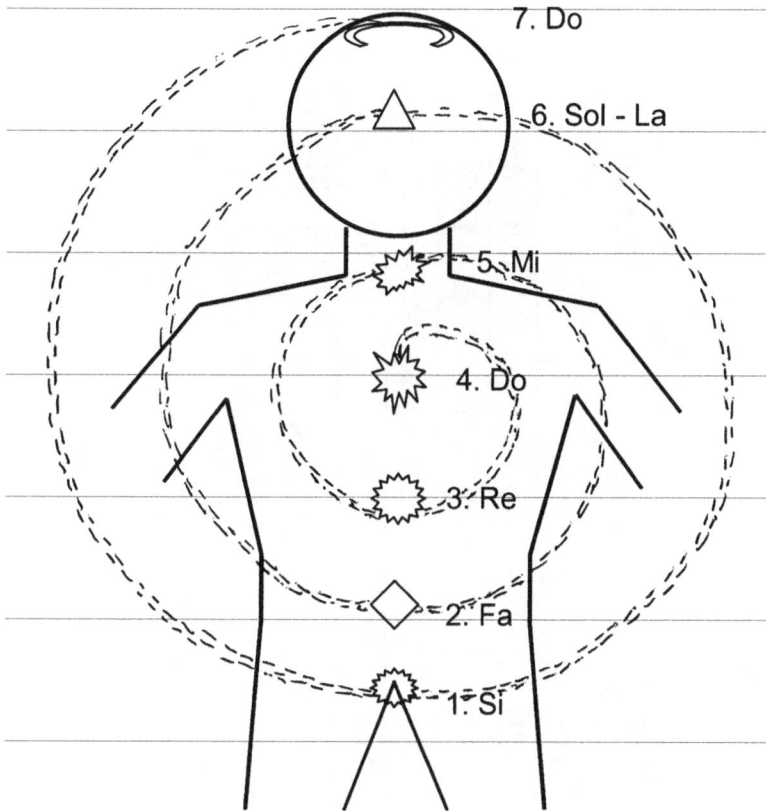

Figure 5-4: Human beings as a cosmos

Table 5-1:

The association between the solar system and the human body

NOTE	NUMBER	CURRENT CENTERS	PLANET	GLAND
DO	4	4TH	SUN	THYMUS
RE	3	3RD	MOON	PANCEASE
MI	5A	5TH	MERCURY	THYROID
----	5B	5TH	VENUS	PARA-THYROID
FA	2	2ND	MARS	ADRENALS
SOL	6A	6TH	JUPITER	POSTERIOR PITUITARY
LA	6B	6TH	SATURN	ANTERIOR PITUITARY
SI	1	1ST	URANUS	GONADS
DO	7	7TH	NEPTUNE	PINEAL

There are rhythms in our lives that reflect our biological nature against the rhythmic environment in which we live. The moon goes through its phases and the seasons change. The shifting gravitational pull of the moon sets the rhythm of the ocean tides. Is it possible for external cycles, such as the phases of the moon, to influence our biological rhythms?

Peter Whybrow, M.D., is chairperson of psychiatry at the University of Pennsylvania. He is a Fellow of the American Association for the Advancement of Science and Vice Chair of the Scientific Advisory Board of the National Depressive and Manic Depressive Association. In 1979 he wrote, "In adapting over evolutionary time to a periodic environment, animals including man have developed within themselves many sophisticated clock like mechanisms ... Partly innate and partly shaped by the individual's prevailing surroundings, the rhythms serves to keep us functioning at an optimal level in a predictable but ever changing environment."

Biological rhythms synchronize with external rhythms (such as the day-night cycle). However, regulation of the rhythms themselves is internal. Some of the best-known biological rhythms occur on a 24-hour cycle, called Circadian rhythms. They include rhythmic peaks and drops in body temperature, heart rate, blood pressure, blood-sugar levels, and secretions of certain hormones.

Other biological rhythms are composed of shorter cycles of biological activity. These shorter cycles are ultradian rhythms. The regulated patterns of heartbeats and breathing are examples of ultradian rhythms. There are also cycles of activity that take longer than a day to complete. These are Infradian rhythms. An example of this is the female menstrual cycle, which last about 28 days. The shifts in the level of female sex hormones define the female menstrual cycle.

All materials are composed of atoms. In the standard model of particle physics, atoms consist of a positively charged nucleus or sun, with tiny negatively charged planetary electrons revolving around them. These atoms or elements combine to form compounds. Looking at how elements interact, we find active combines with passive in the presence of a catalyst. In a broad way, the metals are active, the metalloids are passive, and air or nitrogen is the mediator.

Dmitri Ivanovich Mendeleyev (1834-1907) was the Russian chemist who developed the periodic table. In 1869, he framed the periodic law in chemistry. This law states that the chemical properties of the elements depend on their relative atomic masses. This law is the basis of the periodic table of the elements. He arranged the elements by atomic number (the total positive charge on the nucleus of an atom), and organized them into related groups. The fully extended periodic table folds into a compact form that shows the division of the elements into three categories (see Table 5-2):

1. The first category is the extremely variable representative elements.

2. The second category is the more similar transition metals.

3. The third category is the virtually identical inner transition elements.

Table 5-2:
The Periodic Table

REPRESENTATIVE ELEMENTGS

NOTE	SI	LA	SOL	FA	-	MI	RE	DO
Group	1	2	3	4	5	6	7	8
Period								
1	1 H							2 He
2	3 Li	4 Be	5 B	6 C	7 N	8 O	9 F	10 Ne
3	11 Na	12 Mg	13 Al	14 Si	15 P	16 S	17 Cl	18 Ar
4	19 K	20 Ca	31 Ga	32 Ge	33 As	34 Se	35 Br	36 Kr
5	37 Rb	38 Sr	49 In	50 Sn	51 Sb	52 Te	53 I	54 Xe
6	55 Cs	56 Ba	81 Tl	82 Pb	83 Bi	84 Po	85 At	86 Rn
7	87 Fr	88 Ra	113 Uut	114 Uuq	115 Uup	116 Uuh	117 Uus	118 Uuo

TRANSITION ELEMENTS

21 Sc	22 Ti	23 V	24 Cr	25 Mn	26 Fe	27 Co	28 Ni	29 Cu	30 Zn
39 Y	40 Zr	41 Nb	42 Mo	43 Tc	44 Ru	45 Rh	46 Pd	47 Ag	48 Cd
71 Lu	72 Hf	73 Ta	74 W	75 Re	76 Os	77 Ir	78 Pt	79 Au	80 Hg
103 Lr	104 Rf	105 Db	106 Sg	107 Bh	108 Hs	109 Mt	110 Ds	111 Uuu	112 Uub

INNER TRANSITION ELEMENTS

57 La	58 Ce	59 Pr	60 Nd	61 Pm	62 Sm	63 Eu	64 Gd	65 Tb	66 Dy	67 Ho	68 Er	69 Tm	70 Yb
89 Ac	90 Th	91 Pa	92 U	93 Np	94 Pu	95 Am	96 Cm	97 Bk	98 Cf	99 Es	100 Fm	101 Md	102 No

The doctrine of reciprocal maintenance gives us a unique understanding of human existence. The possibilities that exist in life are unlimited. Here, people have a threefold nature: a thinking nature, a feeling nature, and an instinctive nature. One way of looking at this concept of a person's possible development is to take Gurdjieff division of human nature into seven categories. Person number one is a pure materialist. They are only worried about their own material needs. Person number two is a person who has a dominant feeling nature. Although more sensitive than person number one, they are still self-centered. Person number three is a person who has a dominant thinking nature. They live by theory, and assess everything in terms of yes or no.

Person number four has learned to balance themselves between their bodies, their feelings, and their thoughts. This is what it means to be a real man or real woman. This is the first step towards liberation from our egos. At this point one sees what is necessary in order to achieve self-actualization and spiritual-fulfillment. In addition, they are willing to make the necessary sacrifices in order to reach their goals. The most important property is that person number four has a "permanent center of gravity". This means a settled and final attitude towards life. They have a system of values, and they live by them.

Person number five is beyond ordinary human existence. They have transformed. They now have a second body. This is what the Theosophists (a mystical religious philosophy that goes back to ancient times) called the astral body. This astral body is capable of leaving the nature body for an out-of-body experience.

Person number six has reached a stage where they are concerned with the salvation of all creatures. They have transcended to a "Higher-Being-Body." This is the seat of objective reason, which is the principle of immortality. Person number seven has reached the ultimate liberation. They now represent the cosmic reality. This is where the spiritual and the material worlds harmonize.

In summary, the "fourth task" of a person of knowledge and power is to learn to see them self, and the world around them from a universal or cosmological point of view. A true cosmological point of view will allow you to satisfy your threefold nature of body, soul, and spirit (regardless of your religion). Cosmology is the study of the universe in its totality. The study of the universe has a long history involving science, philosophy, and religion.

In modern science, cosmology is the branch of physics and astrophysics that deals with the study of the physical origins of the universe. Science seeks to explain the universe through astronomy and mathematics. In philosophy and metaphysics, cosmology deals with the universe in terms of all phenomena. It addresses questions using logic and reason that are beyond the scope of science. A religious cosmology is a system of beliefs that describe or explain the origin and structure of the universe. This system of beliefs includes human life, and the relationship of human beings to the rest of the universe.

Esoteric cosmology includes many of the same concerns addressed by religious and philosophical cosmologies. This cosmology attempts to integrate the spiritual with the psychological; however, its emphasis is on intellectual understanding rather than faith. Gurdjieff's "Fourth Way" is one example of an esoteric cosmology. Gurdjieff's law of reciprocal maintenance includes an archetypal pattern for the development of all progressions in the universe, including human beings.

In Gurdjieff's system of cosmology, within the Absolute, there are three fundamental forces or laws, which constitute one whole, one consciousness, or one will. The interaction between these three fundamental forces is the cause of all creation. They separate and unite by their own Divine will, and create all phenomena. These modifications to the Absolute represent "The Law of Three."

The next concept in Gurdjieff's system of cosmology is the "Law of Seven," or "Law of Octaves." The notes on a musical scale express the law of octaves in the form of music. The seven notes: do, re, mi, fa, sol, la, si, do form an octave; with the eighth note having a frequency twice that of the first. This represents the relationship between phenomena at all levels of existence from the atom to the universe.

Gurdjieff's doctrine of cosmoses is the archetypal pattern for the development of all progressions in the universe. Cosmoses are individualized states of existence with the same cosmic model. They are current centers or transformers. They transform energy for the purpose of reciprocal maintenance. The Enneagram represents the simplest model of a cosmos, which is the combination of the law of three and the law seven. This combination shows the cosmic relationship betweens grater and lesser cosmoses.

Each individual human being is a cosmos, or center for the transformation of energy for the purpose of reciprocal maintenance. When we apply the combination of the law of three and the law seven to human beings, we see the endocrine system and its products represent the law of octaves, and the three nervous controls represent the law of three. A living cosmos is the simplest model of the interaction of the law of three and the law of seven. The three forces and the seven aspects are different ways of looking at the same phenomenon.

Rexology is about one person's search for truth, knowledge, and understanding. Understanding the knowledge you have acquired gives you the ability to apply it. This ability to apply knowledge makes you "a person of knowledge and power." Becoming a person of knowledge and power is an on going process, or never ending struggle. By definition, a warrior is a person engaged in a struggle or conflict. Because life itself is a struggle, each of us is a warrior by default. This obligates us to live in terms of our values and beliefs.

The main question behind Rexology is, "With all the different thoughts, beliefs, religions, and sciences; how do you know what path to follow in order to find self-actualization (The fulfillment of your total potential) and spiritual-fulfillment (Having values and beliefs, as to right and wrong, such that you are willing to live or die for)?" This book presents "four tasks" that will help you to answer the question behind Rexology:

1. The "first task" is to come to know self.

2. The "second task" is to develop your consciousness.

3. The "third task" is to interact with the world around you on a conscious level.

4. The "fourth task" is to learn to see yourself, and the world around you, from a cosmological point of view.

When you decide to live your life by a certain set of standards, you must not be too hard on yourself if you sometimes fall short. The reality is "people are not perfect." In ordinary life, one must not go to extremes in any area, but rather take life as a whole in moderation. How much is moderate? How far is "too far?" A part of the answer is our awareness to our selves, to others, and to our situations.

The question then becomes, "How does one internalize a particular way of life or philosophy?" First, look at what you are doing. Make a list of how you spend your time. Second, make a list of your objectives. Now compare what you are doing, with what it is you need to do in order to accomplish your objectives. Having decided what is needed, one simply engage in their daily practice, giving what ever they do their full attention. Through this method, we affect both our body and our mind. Over the years, certain changes occur in the way we move, in the way we feel, and in how we think. A kind of physical and mental settling takes place.

The materialist goals of traditional society and the ego-centered lifestyles of ordinary people are obsolete. The emphasis is no longer "I, I, me, me." In this new millennium, a more creative society and a completely new kind of individual will emerge. You have to get rid of the false ideas you hold about yourself and your relationship to the universe. Ignorance is bondage, but knowledge is freedom! You can actually find an identity that goes far beyond all so-called normal limits. This new individual will be a "whole man" or "whole woman" who is free of social conditioning; and not limited by space, time, or circumstances; and who will express love and understanding towards all. For this is the way of Rexology; becoming brave, good, and wise all at the same time.

Index

www.ingramcontent.com/pod-product-compliance
Lightning Source LLC
La Vergne TN
LVHW091155080426
835509LV00006B/690